THEODORE PARKER

Engraving of Theodore Parker from *Prayers of Theodore Parker,* 1882.

THEODORE PARKER

Orator of Superior Ideas

David B. Chesebrough

Foreword by Mark A. Noll

Great American Orators, Number 29
Bernard K. Duffy and Halford R. Ryan, Series Advisers

GREENWOOD PRESS
Westport, Connecticut • London

Library of Congress Cataloging-in-Publication Data

Chesebrough, David B., 1932–
    Theodore Parker : orator of superior ideas / David B. Chesebrough;
    foreword by Mark A. Noll.
        p.   cm. — (Great American orators, ISSN 0898-8277 ; no. 29)
    Includes bibliographical references and index.
    ISBN 0-313-30873-X (alk. paper)
    1. Parker, Theodore, 1810–1860. 2. Preaching—United States—
History—19th century. 3. Unitarian churches—United States—
Clergy—Biography. 4. Orators—United States—Biography.
5. Unitarian churches—Sermons. 6. Sermons, American. I. Title.
II. Series.
BV4208.U6C48   1999
289.1'092—dc21
[B]   98–47760

British Library Cataloguing in Publication Data is available.

Library of Congress Catalog Card Number: 98–47760
ISBN: 0-313-30873-X
ISSN: 0898-8277

First published in 1999

Greenwood Press, 88 Post Road West, Westport, CT 06881
An imprint of Greenwood Publishing Group, Inc.
www.greenwood.com

Printed in the United States of America

∞™

The paper used in this book complies with the
Permanent Paper Standard issued by the National
Information Standards Organization (Z39.48–1984).

10 9 8 7 6 5 4 3 2 1

Copyright Acknowledgments

The author and publisher are grateful for excerpts from *The Transcendentalists: An Anthology* by
Perry Miller. Copyright © 1950 by the President and Fellows of Harvard College. Reprinted by per-
mission of Harvard University Press.

Every reasonable effort has been made to trace the owners of copyright materials in this book, but
in some instances this has proven impossible. The author and publisher will be glad to receive information leading to more complete acknowledgments in subsequent printings of the book and in the
meantime extend their apologies for any omissions.

For

Sharon Hagan Foiles

With an appreciation beyond

what mere words can express

Contents

Series Foreword

The idea for a series of books on great American orators grew out of the recognition that there is a paucity of book-length studies on individual orators and their speeches. Apart from a few notable exceptions, the study of American public address has been pursued in scores of articles published in professional journals. As helpful as these studies have been, none has or can provide a complete analysis of a speaker's rhetoric. Book-length studies, such as those in this series, will help fill the void that has existed in the study of American public address and its related disciplines of politics and history, theology and sociology, communication and law. In a book, the critic can explicate a broader range of a speaker's persuasive discourse than reasonably could be treated in an article. The comprehensive research and sustained reflection that books require will undoubtedly yield many original and enduring insights concerning the nation's most important voices.

Public address has been a fertile ground for scholarly investigation. No matter how insightful their intellectual forebears, each generation of scholars must reexamine its universe of discourse, while expanding the compass of its researches and redefining its purpose and methods. To avoid intellectual torpor new scholars cannot be content simply to see through the eyes of those who have come before them. We hope that this series of books will stimulate important new understandings of the nature of persuasive discourse and provide opportunities for scholarship in the history and criticism of American public address.

This series examines the role of rhetoric in the United States. American speakers shaped the destiny of the colonies, the young republic, and the mature nation. During each stage of intellectual, political, and religious development of the United States, great orators, standing at the rostrum, on the stump, and in the pulpit, used words and gestures to influence their audiences. Usually striving for the noble, sometimes achieving the base, they urged their fellow citizens toward a more perfect Union. The books in this series chronicle and explain the accomplishments of representative American leaders as orators.

A series of book-length studies on American persuaders honors the role men and women have played in U.S. history. Previously, if one desired to assess the impact of a speaker or a speech upon history, the path was, at best, not well marked and, at worst, littered with obstacles. To be sure, one might turn to biographies and general histories to learn about an orator, but for the public address scholar these sources often prove unhelpful. Rhetorical topics, such as speech invention, style, delivery, organizational strategies, and persuasive effect, are often treated in passing, if mentioned at all. Authoritative speech texts are often difficult to locate, and the problem of textual accuracy is frequently encountered. This is especially true for those figures who spoke one or two hundred years ago or for those whose persuasive role, though significant was secondary to other leading lights of the age.

Each book in this series is organized to meet the needs of scholars and students of the history and criticism of public address. Part I is a critical analysis of the orator and his or her speeches. Within the format of a case study, one may expect considerable latitude. For instance, in a given chapter an author might explicate a single speech or a group of related speeches, or examine orations that comprise a genre of rhetoric such as forensic speaking. But the critic's focus remains on the rhetorical considerations of speaker, speech, occasion, and effect. Part II contains the texts of important addresses that are discussed in the critical analysis that precedes it. To the extent possible, each author has endeavored to collect authoritative speech texts, which have often been found through original research in collections of primary source material. In a few instances, because of the extreme length of a speech, texts have been edited, but the authors have been careful to delete material that is least important to the speech, and these deletions have been held to a minimum.

In each book there is a chronology of major speeches that serves more purposes than may be apparent at first. Pragmatically, it typically lists all of the orator's known speeches and addresses. Places and dates of the speeches are also listed, although this is information that is sometimes difficult to determine precisely. But in a wider sense, the chronology attests to the scope of rhetoric in the United States. Certainly in quantity if not always in quality, Americans are historically talkers and listeners.

Because of the disparate nature of the speakers examined in this series, there is some latitude in the nature of the bibliographical materials that have been included in each book. But in every instance, authors have carefully described original historical materials and collections and gathered critical studies, biographies and autobiographies, and a variety of secondary sources that bear on the speaker and the oratory. By combining in each book bibliographical materials, speech texts, and critical chapters, this series notes that text and research sources are interwoven in the act of rhetorical criticism.

May the books in this series serve to memorialize the nation's greatest orators.

Bernard K. Duffy
Halford R. Ryan

Foreword

Theodore Parker lived in an age of greater-than-life Americans. A contemporary of Daniel Webster, Henry Clay, and Abraham Lincoln, as well as a personal friend of John Quincy Adams and many of the leading religious leaders of the northeastern states, Parker knew up close many of the individuals who have always featured large in the American antebellum era. It is, however, one of the defects of antebellum history as it is so often written for students and other interested readers that Theodore Parker does not occupy a larger place.

Parker was a person of seemingly unmeasurable energy. Like at least some other consumptives, he packed more into his relatively short life than most ordinary people do in their three score and ten or more. It might be said of Parker as has been remarked about some voluble spirits of our own age, that he never had an unrecorded thought. But in Parker's case, this was not such a bad thing, for his thoughts were uniformly fresh, usually informative, and often ethically challenging. Even people who did not agree with his Unitarian religion, his ardent efforts on behalf of social reform, or his stance on the political issues that led to the Civil War could agree that what Parker said carried weight. Parker was not a polemical attack dog in the manner of some modern celebrities known for their verbal pyrotechnics. To be sure, he was an extremely self-confident person. Indeed, those who continued to hold on to some of the religious or social opinions that Parker discarded considered him stunningly, even recklessly self-confident. Some who read about him today will come to the same conclusion. Yet even those who cannot agree with what Parker affirmed must admit that how he said what he said was truly remarkable.

Yet precisely the manner of Parker's speaking has been strangely neglected in previous accounts of his life. The genuine contribution of David Chesebrough's fine study of Parker as orator is to demonstrate with learned but accessible prose how important Parker's mode of address actually was. It might seem tangential to write an *oratorical* study of a major American figure. No judgment could be further from the truth for Theodore Parker. As he spoke so he existed. As he existed so he spoke. Parker's sermonizing as a regular minster, his lecturing to hundreds of audiences during the height of his career, and his speechifying on behalf of several moral causes defined who he was and why he was so important to his times. The keen insight of Chesebrough's book is to show that a study of Parker the orator is the very best entrance into his life. Whether preaching the sermons for which he was both beloved and hated, instructing his countrymen on their religious and civic duties, making the public arguments on behalf of slavery and other social problems that won him an incredible amount of attention, or expostulating on subjects in biography, literature, and general history, the orator was the essential person. Even Parker's writings, some of which were of consequence in fields as far afield as biblical criticism or the meaning of human passions, read like speeches. Chesebrough's work on Parker the orator is, thus, a fuller study of the man than one might first expect.

It is also a study that opens up the era and the place in which Parker lived. Parker was a key player in the definition of Unitarianism vis-a-vis America's most traditional Protestant denominations and in the great internal divisions within Unitarianism during the decades before the Civil War. His church in Boston drew one of the largest congregations in the nation to hear him preach. He played a key role in heating Northern moral passion over slavery. His response to events like the Mexican War, the Fugitive Slave Act, and the fruitless effort to find a political compromise during the 1850s marked him out as one of the nation's leading social commentators. He was a central figure in the life of Boston at a time when that city still dominated the elite intellectual culture of the entire nation. Many, many people of high estate and low commented on his speeches (commentary that Chesebrough turns to good account). His skill with metaphors was not only widely admired but also widely imitated (how Parker's metaphors may have shaped Abraham Lincoln's own discourse is nicely described in the pages that follow). And he was not afraid to talk about any subject before any group.

In a word, to study Parker's speeches and the settings in which he made them is to study a whole lot of important American history and to encounter a great number of extraordinarily interesting American citizens. Once again, the focus on Theodore Parker as an orator might seem like work done in a corner, but in fact it illuminates a huge canvas.

One more word is in order about the structure of Chesebrough's book. The first half is a graceful insightful introduction to this important life. The scholarly apparatus at the end includes a helpful bibliography and a very important chronology of Parker's most noteworthy public addresses (it is by itself a mini-chronicle of momentous American decades). In between the biographical introduction and the scholarly wrap-up come Chesebrough's presentation and commentary upon three of Parker's most important addresses. By the time readers arrive at this point in the book, they will be more than ready to enjoy these speeches. In them and in Chesebrough's expert commentary they will not be disappointed. They are a fitting climax to this exceedingly engaging volume, for they let you feel almost what it was like to have been thee.

Mark A. Noll
Professor of History
Wheaton College

Acknowledgments

I wish to express my appreciation to various members of the Greenwood Press staff who have been so helpful and encouraging in the publication of this book. First, there is Pamela St. Clair, acquisitions editor, with whom I began correspondence on this work, and who throughout production has always been gracious, courteous and prompt in answering the many queries I have posed to her. To Nicholas Kosar goes much of the credit for the formatting and the appearance of the book.

Dr. Halford Ryan, one of the co-editors of the Great American Orator Series, made several suggestions after reading the original manuscript. This is a better book because of his suggestions. Of course, he shares no responsibility for any weaknesses this volume may have.

I am greatly indebted to Dr. Mark Noll, professor of history at Wheaton College, for writing the foreword for this volume. He truly understands the importance of Theodore Parker in our nation's history.

Finally, and most importantly, there is Sharon Hagan Foiles. Since 1991, I have had the good fortune to experience the publication of five books. This would not have been accomplished without Sharon's help. Her technological skills are what makes my manuscripts look good. She has always rendered this aid with a kindly spirit without making me feel like the technological idiot that I really am. I am greatly indebted to her, and as a small way of expressing my appreciation, this book is dedicated to her.

Introduction

The mid-nineteenth century was the golden age of American oratory, both in quantity and quality. The United States Senate has never included the number of rhetorical giants as it did then: John C. Calhoun, Henry Clay, Stephen Douglas, William Graham Sumner, and Daniel Webster. There was another politician with extraordinary oratorical skills, who served for a brief time in the House of Representatives and later in a higher office, by the name of Abraham Lincoln. The abolitionist movement added its own names to the oratorical hall of fame: Frederick Douglass, Wendell Phillips, Theodore Dwight Weld, and the illiterate but extremely effective former slave, Sojourner Truth. In addition to Sojourner Truth, there were other women whose rhetoric moved the people of those times, especially on behalf of women's suffrage and other rights, such as Elizabeth Cady Stanton and Susan B. Anthony. The clergy, as they do in every era, made their own contributions to oratorical greatness: Henry Ward Beecher, whom one biographer has labeled as "our first, self-appointed national chaplain;"[1] Phillips Brooks; Charles Grandison Finney, "the father of modern revivalism;" and the southern minister who championed slavery and secession, Benjamin Morgan Palmer. Add to this list the names of Ralph Waldo Emerson, Edward Everett, and several others who should be included, and one begins to wonder if ever there was a period in American history when the nation had so many individuals who so excelled in what they said and how they said it. No ghost writers, no speech mechanics, for these orators. Though all of them borrowed ideas and phrases from numerous sources, including each other, they arranged the material in their own unique ways and delivered their discourses in a manner that best suited their individual personalities.

Another name from the mid-nineteenth century that must be added to the list of oratorical giants, a name that is equal to any of the above when rhetorical talent is considered, and surpassing many of them, is that of Theodore Parker, the Unitarian minister from Boston. Parker was a superior public speaker, in spite of traits that might have dictated otherwise. "He had no tricks of oratory," Henry Steele Commager has appraised, "his voice was harsh, his gestures awkward, he lectured from a manuscript, but he was one of the greatest orators of his generation." Commager continued:

He did not condescend to his audience, but gave them the hard, gritty truth, and learning too. He could marshall his facts like an army and maneuver them with brilliance. He handled words superbly, no polish, no subtlety, but an elemental force, a vividness of imagery, a richness of texture that no one could match, not even Phillips, not even Beecher.[2]

It was through orations that Parker most influenced his times. It is imperative to note, however, that Parker was an important writer as well as an orator. In 1843 he translated from the German language Wilhelm M. L. De Witte's classical two-volume work, *A Critical and Historical Introduction to the Canonical Scriptures of the Old Testament*. Parker biographer Robert Albrecht described the translation as "a significant achievement showing immense erudition; few, if any, other Americans could have done it."[3] Other books would follow, most of which were publications of previous orations or compilations of ideas that he had previously expressed through speech. Parker aided Emerson, Alcott, and Fuller in founding *The Dial*, a Transcendental paper, to which he contributed several articles. He served for a time with Emerson and J. E. Cabot as co-editor of the *Massachusetts Quarterly Review*, and then briefly as the sole editor and principle writer. He even wrote poetry, quite a bit of it, some of it good, none of it superior. His correspondence was prodigious. He once communicated to William Herndon, Abraham Lincoln's law partner in Springfield, Illinois, of writing one thousand letters over a five month period. John White Chadwick, a biographer, has commented on those letters.

Parker's [letters] were of many kinds. There were little notes among them, but what is truly remarkable is the number of letters containing thousands of words and great masses of careful exegesis and elaborate information. The multitude of his letters and correspondents is far less impressive than the prodigality with which he poured himself forth, the patience with which he answered questions which were often trivial, the faithfulness with which he kept up correspondence with strangers whom he would fain enlighten or encourage, year after year.[4]

John Weiss, a noted scholar on the life and works of Parker, has written: "Few public men ever sustained such a wide and varied correspondence as he."[5] Some of that correspondence was with the most celebrated names of the times, names that included Charles Francis Adams, George Bancroft, John Brown, Salmon P. Chase, Ralph Waldo Emerson, President Millard Fillmore, Margaret Fuller, John P. Hale, Horace Mann, Elizabeth Peabody, George Ripley, William

Seward, Gerrit Smith, and Charles Sumner. The correspondence with Sumner was voluminous. Other correspondence included the governors of some of the states, and exchanges with clergymen and scholars throughout the world.

Parker planned to do more writing, much more, but his early death due to consumption when he was only forty-nine doomed those writing plans. The world is poorer for that. He had so much to share, so much to teach to his and future generations. Notes had been gathered and numerous volumes had been planned in theology, philosophy, and history that would never be. It is doubtful, however, that Parker would have reversed his priorities, whereby oratory would have become secondary to writing, even if he could have predicted his untimely death. Chadwick has written that "the preacher in him was too overpowering to permit a brother near the throne. . . . His sermon style, loose, copious, expansive, eloquent,—was too ungirt, diffuse, redundant for the printed page." Continuing, Chadwick noted, if Parker had given attention and time to the writing he planned, he "would have spoiled two better men."

Theodore Parker, "the great American preacher," as he is justly named upon his monument in Florence, and Theodore Parker, the great ally—one of the greatest—of Garrison and Lincoln in the emancipation of four million slaves. To those two great parts he could not have added that of creative scholarship without marring all.[6]

Parker himself claimed that through his writings he attracted the attention of hundreds, but through his oratory, thousands were enlightened, challenged, stimulated, and changed. Parker believed that scholars, such as himself, had a duty to speak to the masses, to share their lofty thoughts and findings in a manner that common people could comprehend. "It is easy to discourse with scholars," he said, "and in the old academic carriage drive through the broad gateway of the cultivated class, but here the man of genius is to take the new thought on his shoulders and climb up the stiff, steep hill, and find his way where the wild asses quench their thirst, and the untamed eagle builds his nest. Our American scholar must cultivate the dialectics of speech as well as of thought. . . . Thought without power of speech finds little welcome here."[7]

This work is divided into two parts. Part I will sketch the life of Theodore Parker with special emphasis placed upon the development and use of his oratorical skills. Important sermons and speeches will be introduced and quotations from several inserted into the biographical narrative. Chapter 1 will serve as a prologue placing Parker within the larger context of mid-nineteenth century preaching. Chapter 2 will focus on Parker's early years (1810–1841); the influence of his parents, his education and insatiable desire for knowledge, his time at the Harvard Divinity School, the influence of Transcendentalism on his thinking processes, his development of an intuitional theology, and his experiences during his first pastorate at West Roxbury, Massachusetts. Some of the sermons preached over Parker's nine years at West Roxbury will be observed, and through those sermons it will be noted how the young preacher became increasingly more liberal, controversial, and his rhetoric more refined.

Chapter 3 will be concerned with the most important years of Parker's life, the years of influence (1841–1859). Special attention will be devoted to Parker's work and rhetoric in the areas of theological and ecclesiastical reform, social reform, and biographical topics. The chapter will take note of the various rhetorical techniques employed by the mature orator. Parker stressed the importance of "superior ideas," and the necessity of much reading and study to assure he would have something worthwhile to say. For Parker, the organization of material was fundamental, and he criticized other renowned orators of his time for lack of order in their discourses. Parker's use of metaphors and illustrations; his reliance upon intuition rather than the Bible as his source of authority; his emphasis upon sentiments and passion; his insistence that a discourse must fit the audience to which it is addressed; and the importance of being natural, not ostentatious, in delivery, will all be examined. Descriptions from those who heard Parker will reveal much about his style and the effect he had on others.

Chapter 4 will deal with the final months of Parker's life (1859–1860); his final sermon, his attempt to regain his health in Europe, and his death in Florence, Italy. Even in these waning months, a dying and weakened Parker exerted great energy, especially through his writings, to make a moral difference in the world.

In Part II, three Parker sermons/speeches will be recorded in their entirety, or nearly so: "A Sermon of Slavery" (1841), "The Mexican War" (1849), and "The Revival of Religion Which We Need" (1858). Each discourse will be preceded by introductory remarks including a brief analysis of the text.

It is fortunate that so much of what Parker wrote—sermons, addresses, books, articles, letters, poems—has been preserved. These writings, for the most part, can be located in one of three sources: *The Collected Works of Theodore Parker*, a fourteen-volume set, edited by Francis P. Cobbe (1863); *Life and Correspondence of Theodore Parker*, a two-volume work by John Weiss (1864); and the *Centenary Edition of the Works of Theodore Parker*, fifteen volumes, published by the American Unitarian Association (1907–1910).

Theodore Parker is a man who deserves attention as one of the great orators in American history. He had his failings, as all people do,—impatience, perhaps a certain intellectual arrogance, harshness—but these weaknesses, if that they are, were minuscule when compared to his virtues: an unquenchable love of learning that he generously shared with others through his oratory and writings; a work ethic that would have exhausted most others, and eventually did exhaust Parker himself; indomitable courage, a shining sincerity, selflessness, and a great love and appreciation for other human beings, especially those on the lower rungs of society's ladder.

PART I

THE DEVELOPMENT OF AN ORATOR

1

Prologue:
A Mid-Nineteenth-Century Preacher

The mid-nineteenth century brought with it intellectual developments that challenged and sometimes shattered the spiritual foundations of American culture. Science was more and more replacing concepts of divine intervention with natural laws. The new science demanded an exacting methodology for deriving truth, a method calling for observation, experiment, and verification, in place of unchallenged revelation. A climate of opinion arose in several quarters in which materialism, naturalism, and skepticism flourished. Some even began to announce that the age of science had replaced the age of faith. These emerging forces were at best indifferent to religion, at worst openly hostile. Religion was on the defensive as the gap widened between static creeds and a dynamic changing world view. A critical scientific method challenged uncritical religious dogma.

Clergymen differed as to how to respond to these new challenges. Some chose to ignore the challenges, not wanting to draw attention to anything that questioned the unquestionable. Other clergymen chose to fight back by declaring the new discoveries and methodologies as being anti-God, anti-Bible, and anti-spiritual. A third type of clerical response declared that religion must adjust and change in order to incorporate the findings of science into religious truth. Theodore Parker was among the most prominent of American preachers to be found in this latter group. It was time, declared Parker, if religion was to be preserved, to re-examine all religious dogma and to raise questions about those matters thought to be beyond questioning; the Church and its teachings, the scriptures, and even the divinity of Christ. Other noteworthy preachers of the era found different means of accommodation. Henry Ward Beecher, the most popular preacher in mid-nineteenth century America, was instrumental in the declaration of ways to reconcile the new science and the old faith. The famous evangelist, Charles G. Finney, introduced a new theology and methodology into revivalism. Phillips Brooks, the gifted Episcopal rector, made dogma and sectarianism secondary to addressing the needs of people. It was Theodore Parker, however, who was the most radical in his demands for and practice of ecclesiastical change.

By the mid-nineteenth century, sermons were still lengthy by today's standards. It was not until the latter part of the century that sermons began to shorten. Those long sermons were indicative of the fact that preaching still held a high priority in Protestant churches. Parker's sermons were often two hours in length. Gaius Glen Atkins, a scholar of nineteenth-century homiletics, has written that for "both the preacher and for the congregation, such sermons as these were the events of the week, prepared laboriously and lovingly by the preacher, awaited eagerly by the congregation. A sermon was in those days," affirmed Atkins, "a creation of the artist-prophet and an end in itself. These preachers went to their pulpits as to thrones."[1]

For the most part, nineteenth-century sermons were the products of creative and well-informed minds. The preachers were widely read in diverse fields. They knew theology, but they also knew what was taking place in science and what had happened in history. Philosophy and classical studies were an important part of their training. As they created their orations they drew from a wide range of resources. Atkins has drawn a contrast between those sermons of the mid-nineteenth century and those of the mid-twentieth century, some one hundred years later.

Modern preaching is brighter, quicker in movement, more concerned for the interest-content and possibly more projective. But one might as well admit first as last that, compared with these [nineteenth-century] sermons, most now-published sermons are thin. . . . [Nineteenth-century sermons] at their best, glow with a sustained and creative passion. They possess an inner skeletal integrity and rise at intervals to a noble eloquence. They lack the modern psychological techniques but they know human nature and touch its faults and failures with uncanny insight.[2]

Parker's ministry covered a span of twenty-two years (1837–1859) during which he wrote 925 sermons and preached approximately 1,500 times. For the last fifteen years of his ministry the weekly congregations at the Music Hall in Boston numbered about 3,000.[3] Only Henry Ward Beecher, of the Plymouth Congregational Church in Brooklyn, commanded a larger audience.[4]

It was not just in ecclesiastical settings that Parker spoke. He gave orations at educational conferences, at temperance, women's rights, and antislavery meetings, and filled his calendar with engagements on the Lyceum lecture circuit. During the winter season it was not unusual for Parker to fill fourteen lyceum appointments a month in addition to his Sunday sermons which he seldom missed, and felt guilty if he did. These lectures sent Parker into villages and cities throughout New England. He would often go to Pennsylvania and New York, and sometimes as far away as Illinois and Wisconsin. Everywhere he went, great crowds of men and women came to hear this man expound on some great moral issue of the day or to hear his ideas on various topics that were a part of his prodigious learning. In a final letter to his Boston congregation, an extremely ill Theodore Parker recalled his experiences on the lecture circuit.

Since 1848, I have lectured eighty or a hundred times each year,—in every Northern State east of the Mississippi, once also in a Slave State, and on Slavery itself. I have taken most exciting and important subjects, of the greatest concern to the American people, and treated them independent of sect or party, street or press, and with what learning and talent I could command. I put the manner in quite various forms—for each audience is made up of many. For eight or ten years, on the average, I have spoken to sixty or a hundred thousand persons in each year, besides addressing you on Sundays, in the great Hall you threw open to all comers.

Thus I have had a wide field of operation, where I might arouse the Sentiment of Justice and Mercy, diffuse such Ideas as I thought needful for the welfare and progress of the people, and prepare for such Action as the occasion might one day require.[5]

Parker estimated that he lectured to sixty thousand people each year over a ten-year period. He declared that he hoped he had made a strong impression on one half of one percent of that audience, or 3,000 per year.[6] Whether in sermons or lectures, Parker pressed for change and reform; reform in theology and ecclesiology, and reform in the social arena. No one demands such sweeping and radical change without incurring strong and sometimes vicious opposition. In that final letter to his beloved congregation, Parker recalled some of the opposition he had faced.

I had been ecclesiastically reported to the People as a "Disturber of the public peace," "an infidel," "an Atheist," "an enemy to mankind." When I was to lecture in a little town, the minister, even the Unitarian, commonly stayed at home. Many, in public or private, warned their followers "against listening to that bad man. Don't look him in the face!" Others stoutly preached against me. So, in the Bar-room "I was the song of the drunkard," and the minister's text in the Pulpit. But, when a few hundreds, in a mountain town of New England, or in some settlement on a prairie of the West, or, when many hundreds, in a wide city, did look me in the face, and listen for an hour or two while I spoke, plain, right-on, of matters familiar to their patriotic hopes, their business and their bosoms, as their faces glowed in the excitement of what they heard, I saw the clerical prejudice was stealing out of their mind, and I left them other than I found.[7]

What a marked contrast between Parker and Henry Ward Beecher, the most popular preacher of the era. Parker was out in front, way out in front, on almost everything; Beecher was almost always cautious about flying in the face of the prevailing winds of public opinion. Paxton Hibben, in a critical biography of Beecher, asserts that Beecher tested the moods of his congregations and adjusted his stance accordingly, that he struck at slavery only after it was safe to do so. Hibben charges that Beecher was a "barometer and record" of the social mood. "He made no one uncomfortable, least of all himself. . . . He was not in advance of his day, but precisely abreast of his day."[8] Though Hibben may have overstated his criticism of Beecher, no such judgments could ever be justifiably leveled at Parker. Parker never, just because someone might be offended, refrained from speaking his mind, from uttering what he thought to be the truth, or declaring his views on the morality or immorality of various issues. Parker has been accused—perhaps with some justification—of harboring certain vices: impatience, insensitivity, harshness, a bent towards radicalism, and intellectual arrogance. He never, however, could be charged with cowardice, timidity, or compromising on truth or ethics.

It was not that Parker failed to care about what people thought of him. He did care and was often reduced to tears because of the harsh remarks and criticisms of others. Though some may have perceived him as being insensitive, that was not the truth and he was deeply pained by the slurs and the shunning from others. On one occasion Parker wrote to a friend, "I am the best-hated man in the land."[9] Though there would seem to be a certain self-pity, even hyperbole, in the remark, one cannot help but surmise that he also took a certain pride in a designation that truly set him apart from others.

Parker strongly believed that scholars, people of intellect, like himself, had an obligation to share their findings and discoveries, through speech, with the common masses. "The man of genius," he emphasized, "is to take the new thought on his shoulders and climb up the stiff, steep hill, and find his way where the wild asses quench their thirst, and the untamed eagle builds its nest. Our American scholar must cultivate the dialectics of speech as well as of thought."[10]

Parker's training in rhetoric had a classical basis. Near the end of his life he wrote: "Here [in the *English State Trials*] and in the Greek and Latin orations I got the best part of my rhetorical culture."[11] Other volumes that influenced his rhetorical style were Campbell's *Philosophy of Rhetoric*, Whately's *Elements of Rhetoric*, and Adams's *Lectures on Rhetoric and Oratory*.[12]

2

The Early Years (1810–1841)

Theodore Parker was born on August 24, 1810, in Lexington, Massachusetts, not far from that place where the "shots heard round the world" were fired. Theodore Parker's grandfather, Captain John Parker, was an important part of that first battle of the American Revolution, for it was he who commanded the company of Lexington minutemen. Early in the morning of April 19, 1775, as a squadron of British troops approached, some of Parker's men began to waver; whereupon the captain ordered them to stand their ground and threatened to shoot any man who left his post. As the British drew near, the captain called out, "Don't fire unless fired upon; but if they mean to have war, let it begin here!"[1] And so it began. Captain John Parker's courage, determination, and a passion to achieve what he thought was right, regardless of the cost involved, were characteristics passed on to his famous grandson, Theodore.

The town of Lexington in which Theodore Parker spent his early years was in a rural setting. The wonders and beauty of nature were everywhere; expansive fields, woods, flowers, unpolluted skies, streams and ponds, domestic and wild animals, along with the fish of the waters—all to be found within the changing settings of the four seasons. The young Parker sensed the presence of God in nature, and later sermons and addresses would be filled with references to the joy and spirituality found in the creation.

He was the youngest of eleven children, the only one in the family to achieve eminence. His mother Hannah and his father John both made significant contributions to the formulation of their eleventh offspring. Though Hannah died when Theodore was only thirteen, she lived long enough to impart concepts and values that would become vitally important to her son in later years. In the following paragraph, from an autobiographical fragment written near the end of his life, Parker described his mother's religion, characteristics of which would all find their way into his own theology.

She was eminently a religious woman. I have known few in whom the religious instincts were so active and profound, and who seemed to me to enjoy so completely the life of God in the soul of man. To her the Deity was an Omnipresent Father, filling every point of space with His beautiful and loving presence. She saw Him in the rainbow, and in the drops of rain which helped to compose it as they fell into the muddy ground, to come up grass and trees, and corn and flowers. She took a deep and still delight in silent prayer—of course it was chiefly the more spiritual part of the Old Testament and New Testament that formed her favorite reading; the dark theology of the times seems not to have stained her soul at all. She took great pains with the moral culture of her children, at least with mine.[2]

Parker would develop a theology based upon intuitive truth. Authority and truth had their ultimate sources, not in the Church nor in the Bible, but in conscience, which Parker often referred to as the voice of God or higher law. It was a concept, as will be later seen, that caused many to label Parker a heretic. It was also a concept he learned first from his mother. Parker wrote of an incident that happened when he was four years of age and the impact of that incident upon his life.

When a little boy in petticoats in my fourth year, one fine day in spring, my father led me by the hand to a distant part of the farm, but soon sent me home alone. On the way I had to pass a little "pond-hole" then spreading its waters wide; a rhodora in full bloom—a rare flower in my neighborhood, and which grew only in that local-ity—attracted my attention and drew me to the spot. I saw a little spotted tortoise sunning itself in the shallow water at the root of the flaming shrub. I lifted the stick in my hand to strike the harmless reptile; for, though I had never killed any creature, yet I had seen other boys out of sport destroy birds, squirrels, and the like, and I felt a disposition to follow their example. But all at once something checked my little arm, and a voice within me said, clear and loud, "It is wrong!" I held my uplifted stick in wonder at the new emotion—the consciousness of an involuntary but inward check upon my actions—till the tortoise and the rhodora both vanished from my sight. I hastened home and told the tale to my mother, and asked what was it that told me it was wrong? She wiped a tear from her eye with her apron, and taking me in her arms, said, "Some men call it conscience, but I prefer to call it the voice of God in the soul of man. If you listen and obey it, then it will speak clearer, and always guide you right; but if you turn a deaf ear or disobey, then it will fade out little by little, and leave you all in the dark and without a guide. Your life depends on heeding this little voice." She went her way, careful and troubled about many things, but doubtless pondered them in her motherly heart; while I went off to wonder and think it over in my poor childish way. But I am sure no event in my life has made so deep and lasting an impression on me.[3]

Because his mother's religious and moral influence was so profound, it is not surprising that Parker, in later public prayers and sermons, often referred to God as "Our Father and our Mother." His mother's religious influence would overcome other religious influences—"the dark theology of the times"—in the young Parker's life. The *New England Primer*, one of his early schoolbooks, contained, Parker recalled, "ghastly" concepts of God and the Devil. A journal entry in 1839 records the fears of eternal damnation in his early years.

I can hardly think without a shudder of the terrible effect the doctrine of eternal damnation had on me. How many, many hours have I wept with terror as I lay on my bed, till, between praying and weeping, sleep gave me repose. But before I was nine years old this fear went away, and I saw clearer light in the goodness of God. But for years, say from seven till ten, I said my prayers with much devotion, I think, and then continued to repeat, "Lord, forgive my sins," till sleep came on me.[4]

The influence of Theodore's father was of a different kind than that of his mother's, but of at least equal importance. It was his father who taught young Theodore the importance of developing the intellect. John Parker set the example of intellectual pursuit for the family by reading books of substance in history, political economy, and mental philosophy. The family's library contained three hundred volumes, mostly classics.[5] Throughout his life the gifts Parker received from his parents—religious and moral gifts from his mother, intellectual gifts from his father—would become his most important assets.

His early formal schooling was limited to four months of two summers and three months of ten winters in district schools taught by college students, and a few months in Lexington Academy. For much of his education he was self-taught. In the district schools he was far in advance of his peers, having read translations of Homer and Plutarch before he was eight, and Rollins on ancient history at about the same time. Other histories soon followed. He read almost all the poetry he could find and developed a talent for writing his own. A single reading of a poem from five hundred to one thousand lines was sufficient to commit it to memory. When Parker was ten, William H. White, who would one day become a Unitarian minister, took an interest in the precocious child and began to train him in the ancient languages of Greek and Latin. Forty years later, Parker in correspondence to White, continued to express his gratitude for White's disciplined drilling of his student in those ancient languages. Parker taught himself the modern languages. The lad borrowed books from many sources: public libraries, teachers, scholars who knew of his potential, and nearby colleges. Shortly before his twelfth birthday Parker became interested in astronomy and metaphysics. When he was twelve, Parker purchased his first book, a Latin dictionary, with money he earned from picking blackberries. Among the thousands of books he would later acquire, the Latin dictionary would always have an honored place in his library, as it does today in the Boston Public Library to which he willed his books.

At seventeen Parker began four years of teaching in nearby district schools. In 1831 he was invited to teach at a private school in Boston. It was an exalted calling for a young man, scarcely twenty-one, without a college degree, asked to teach in an important school in the great city of Boston. So much was expected of him; he was to teach Latin, Greek, French, mathematics, and philosophy. Lacking confidence in his mathematical skills, Parker received tutoring on the subject to compensate for the self-perceived inadequacy. The many libraries throughout the city were available to him, and, with eagerness and delight, he devoured hundreds of the books upon the many shelves. During this year in Boston "he read all of Homer and much of Xenophon, Demosthenes, and Aeschylus, adding the study of German . . . doing much at the same time in mathematics and philosophy."[6] Considering the ministry as a vocation, he went to listen to several of the renowned preachers in the city. He occasionally attended the Hanover Street Church where the famous Lyman Beecher—father of Henry Ward Beecher—delivered his sermons against Catholicism and Unitarianism, mixed with large doses of brimstone and Calvinism. Beecher had, in fact, been called to Boston from the Mid-West to help slow the tide of a fast-growing Unitarianism. Parker's judgment on Beecher was mixed; some appreciation for style, but no appreciation for substance. "I greatly respected," Parker recalled, "the talents, the zeal, and the enterprise of that able man, who certainly taught me much; but I came away with no confidence in his theology. The better I understood it, the more self-contradictory, unnatural, and hateful did it seem."[7] In future years, Parker would level blistering attacks upon Calvinistic theology, some of those attacks having their roots, no doubt, in those Lyman Beecher sermons. There were some gifted Unitarian preachers in the city whom the young Parker apparently did not hear that first year in Boston: William Ellery Channing at the Federal Street Church, Ralph Waldo Emerson at the Second Church, and George Ripley at the meeting house on Purchase Street. Emerson and Ripley would later abandon the ministry and the church. Parker was disappointed in the Unitarian ministers he did hear, finding them too formal and cold. Though they often challenged the mind, they failed to warm the heart. It was an example that Parker never forgot and would not himself repeat.

In the following year Parker opened a private school in Watertown, not far from Boston. The school, which met over an old bakery, began with two students but soon expanded to fifty-four. It was at Watertown that Parker first encountered racial prejudice. A black girl had to be dismissed from the school because of the strenuous objections of white parents. In later years Parker would look back upon that unfortunate event with shame and self-contempt. He could have done more on the girl's behalf, been more courageous. He would go on, in the future, to more than compensate for this youthful lapse. While at Watertown he "read Cicero, Tacitus, Herodotus, Thucydides, Pindar, Theocritus, Bion, Moschus, Aeschylus; doing much careful translation. Here too, he fell in with Cousin and Jouffroy and Coleridge, and began to lay the foundations of a transcendental system of philosophy."[8]

Parker successfully took the entrance exams to Harvard College. Within a few years he had completed all of his studies with high honors. Because he could not pay the four years of tuition he owed, Harvard would not award him the bachelor's degree. Some years later, in 1840, the college did confer on him an honorary master's degree.

In April of 1834, Parker entered the Harvard Divinity School, beginning his studies in the last term of the junior year. The faculty member who would have the greatest impact on Parker's life was Henry Ware Jr., who taught pulpit eloquence and practical theology at the school. It was Ware, more than any other person, who enabled Parker to become an effective, polished, and powerful orator. It was not an easy task. The young Parker had a roughness that needed refining, a boisterousness that needed taming, a flippancy that needed curbing, and a sense of humor that needed both taste and a sense of appropriate use. But the student was willing to learn and the teacher's persistency would eventually result in dividends far beyond what teacher or pupil could have ever expected. Ware would influence his student in yet another significant way, for Ware was an avowed abolitionist, at a time when abolitionism was considered to be on the radical fringe of American society. Ware's hymn, "Oppression Shall Not Always Reign," became one of the most popular songs of the antislavery movement. Ware was a person who had cultivated for himself sound scholarship and a deep piety, two more characteristics that made a lasting impression upon his student. Years later, Parker wrote of his former teacher, "I loved him as I seldom loved a man heretofore and perhaps shall never love another."[9]

Other instructors at the Divinity School included John Gorham Palfrey, who taught Hebrew and Old Testament Literature, and who, when absent, would ask Parker to take over his Hebrew classes. Palfrey would later gain fame in the antislavery crusade, though he demonstrated little evidence of such an interest when Parker was his student. Andrews Norton was a professor of great influence in the school and an important person of the conservative wing of the Unitarian Church. In future years some bitter theological disputes would erupt between Parker and Norton.

Thirty students attended the Divinity School, and Parker soon knew them all. Some would become close and life-long friends, most especially Samuel P. Andrews. Towards the end of his life, when he was very sick, Parker wrote to Andrews: "I am not well enough to see you—it will make my heart beat too fast."[10] Other students included Christopher Cranch, who gained some notoriety for his poetry and art; George Ellis, who introduced Parker to the transcendental-ist George Ripley; John Dwight, who became closely associated with Brook Farm, another Transcendental influence, and who left the ministry for a career in music; John Parkman, who would become greatly involved in the antislavery movement; Henry Bellows, the eloquent preacher and Unitarian leader who organized the United States Sanitary Commission during the Civil War; Charles Brooks, who became widely recognized for his translations of Goethe and Schiller; Edmund Sears, a poetic mystic who wrote the hymn, "Calm On the Listening Ear of Night;" and several others, each of whom would make his own unique contribution when the seminary days were over. Parker's classmates remembered him as a scholar who far outdistanced the rest of them, a young man of exuberant energy and high spirits. "We all looked upon him," one classmate recalled, "as a prodigious athlete in his studies."[11]

At the beginning of his Divinity School studies, Parker was still fairly orthodox in his theology, at least by Unitarian standards. In a letter to his nephew, Columbus Greene, dated April 2, 1834,—about the time Parker entered the school—the student sought to assure Greene of his orthodoxy.

You inquire about my belief. I believe in the Bible. Does that satisfy you? No, you will say: all Christians profess to the same, and how different they are.

To commence then: I believe there is one God, who has existed from all eternity, with whom the past, present, and future are alike present; that he is almighty, good, and merciful, will reward the good and punish the wicked, both in this life and the next. This punishment may be eternal; of course, I believe that neither the rewards nor punishments of a future state are corporal. Bodily pleasures soon satiate, and may God preserve us from a worse punishment than one's own conscience.

I believe the books of the Old and New Testament to have been written by men inspired by God, for certain purposes, but I do not think them inspired at all times. I believe that Christ was the Son of God, conceived and born in a miraculous manner, that he came to preach a better religion by which man may be saved.

This religion, as I think, allows man the very highest happiness in this life, and promises eternal felicity in another world. I do not think our sins will be forgiven because Christ died. I cannot conceive why they should be, although many good and great men have thought so. I believe God knows all that we shall do, but does not cause us to do anything.[12]

In 1835, his studies in the Old Testament led to beliefs about Jesus that were still quite traditional, but with an important reservation. "I do not doubt," he affirmed, "that Jesus was a man 'sent from God' and endowed with power from on high; that he taught the truth and worked miracles: but that he was the subject of inspired prophecy I very much doubt."[13]

His reading of the Church Fathers caused him to conclude that most of them did far more harm than good.

I am heart-weary and reason-weary of those doting fathers. They have sense, but it is "a grain of wheat in a bushel of chaff " . . . .

Jerome . . . loved glory rather than truth, was superstitious, and an introducer of important errors into the Church, both in doctrine and in interpretation. . . . He was not a profound scholar in Hebrew, or even in Greek. He tasted of theology rather than exhausted it. . . .

St. Augustine, we all know, introduced more error into the Church than any other man. Many of his doctrines fly in the face both of reason and virtue, to extinguish the eyes of one and to stifle the breath of the other. Everybody knows how he persecuted his opposers, Pelagius and Julian, to say nothing of others. . . .

Tertullian . . . first introduced the notion that faith and reason contradict each other. . . . He thought faith which contradicted reason was most acceptable to God.[14]

On July 3, 1836, Parker delivered his first sermon before a congregation other than his peers and faculty at the Divinity School. The following day he wrote of his personal uncertainty about that first preaching experience before "a real live audience." He was also determined to improve.

Last night I preached publicly in Mr. Newell's church. This is the first time in my life that I have preached to a real live audience. I felt much embarrassed, though perhaps it did not show forth. Lydia, my own dear Lydia [his fiancee] and her aunt came over with me. I was less pleased with myself than they were with me. To say the truth, I did not feel the sermon so much as I usually do, for the hour usually spent in preparing for the service was consumed in "doing the agreeable," so I did not get into the sermon so much as commonly.
May God in his mercy grant me power to improve in this holy duty. May I grow from strength to strength, increasing continually in godliness and wisdom, and thus show forth pure and holy Christianity in my life, no less than in my teachings. Oh, God, wilt thou help me to become more pure in heart, more holy and better able to restrain all impetuous desires and unholy passions; may I "put down every high thing" that would exalt itself against the perfect law of God. Help me in the intercourse of life to discharge my duties with a more Christianlike fidelity; to love Thee the more, and those with whom I am to deal![15]

The following month he wrote to Lydia of another preaching experience. The novice orator was obviously gaining in confidence.

I felt somewhat awkward at first, as you may suppose, but I remembered the command, "Now show forth what ye be," and made an effort. I never felt in better spirits for speaking, and not only delivered the written Word, but added much that was better and more reaching extemporaneously.[16]

After graduation from the Divinity School in July 1836, Parker, over the next few months, had the opportunity to preach before several Unitarian congregations in Massachusetts. It would be nine months before a call for a pastorate would be accepted. During this interim period he attended a revival meeting of Methodists at Millennium Grove in Eastham. He strongly disapproved of what he observed and heard. "The women were always the most noisy," he wrote. "Some of them were in hysterics, I should say, and should explain it on well-known physiological principles. They said it was the Spirit. How strangely men mistake the flesh for the Spirit. A twitching of nerves is often mistaken for inspiration."[17] Parker further commented: "I always noticed, too, that the least learned were the most violent—had most of the 'Spirit of the Lord,' as they said. This accounts for the low opinion of learning among them, and for the great power of Whitefield, who was all passion and feeling."[18]
During this same period of time Parker continued, as he would for the rest of his life, a rigorous program of study. He would begin and finish within a year's time a translation from German of DeWette's two-volume work, *Introduction to the Old Testament*, the first primary work of Parker's scholarship. Reading, as it would always be for him, was such an exhilarating experience. "I could devour a whole library in a week," he exaggeratedly explained.[19]
Parker's father died in the late fall of 1836. In a letter to his future wife, the

son expressed his grief and how he intended to deal with his sorrow.

> I had fondly put off the day of his departure, and when the event was told me, my sorrow was tenfold greater than I had anticipated. . . . But how can I, who have been cradled in his arms, led by his hands, blessed by his prayers, and molded by his tender care, how can I forbear lamenting now he is gone?
>
> But enough of this. He is gone. Let us say no more about it; and now I entreat you to say nothing upon that subject in your letters, nor when we meet. A thousand circumstances will bring it all up before me again and again; do not let us multiply them without need.
>
> The valley of tears, if dwelt in, hath a poisonous influence upon the soul; but if only occasionally passed through, it is full of healing waters and fountains of strength.[20]

Most of Parker's correspondence with Lydia was not taken up with melancholy matters. His letters overflowed with joy and devotion for her, sometimes bursting forth in poetry.

> 'Tis sweet, my love, when day is o'er,
> And hushed each jarring sound,
> To turn and think of thee once more;
> It makes my heart rebound.[21]

Some potential pastorates would not open for Theodore Parker. Some feared that his intellectualism would produce incomprehensible sermons. Others were concerned that he might be too liberal, too radical in his views. Rumors were rampant that he was tainted with Transcendentalism, a new and rather undefined term that was used to cover a multitude of heresies. A few harbored doubts about Parker's appearance; not handsome, but plain, a certain awkwardness, and somewhat rustic. Most of those in his graduating class secured positions before he did. In time, however, some flattering offers came from attractive and promising churches. On May 23, 1837, a call was extended from the Spring Street Society at West Roxbury, where he had preached several times, always making a favorable impression. There had been other offers from bigger and more prestigious congregations, with larger salaries, but only the call from West Roxbury attracted Parker. The parish numbered about sixty families, ranging from the fairly wealthy to humble farmers. Though the salary was not large, there were more than ample compensations. The very smallness of the parish would insure adequate time for study. Boston was nearby with its great libraries and giant personalities. It was just what Parker wanted. He accepted the call from West Roxbury and began a nine-year pastorate, and what an eventful and important nine years they would prove to be.

On April 20 he married Lydia Cabot after four years of courtship. It was from every aspect an ideal relationship. Lydia was not Parker's intellectual equal, but few people in the world were. She provided love, in abundance, and for Parker that was the most important element in the world. As he received he also gave. The one blemish in their marriage was that no children were born from it. This was a dark cloud for Parker and he attempted to compensate by enjoying his neighbors' children. After some years in his West Roxbury ministry, by which time his total lack of orthodoxy had been firmly established, Parker said to a neighbor, after playing games with her children, "I am the worst hated man in America, and have no children."²² The relationship with Lydia, however, was always solid. In the early years at West Roxbury, when Lydia was away for a few days, Parker wrote in his journal of his love for and dependence upon her.

At home nominally; but since my wife is gone my home is in New Jersey. I miss her absence—wicked woman!—most exceedingly. I cannot sleep or eat or work without her. It is not so much the affection she bestows on me as that she receives by which I am blessed. I want someone always in the arms of my heart to caress and comfort; unless I have this, I mourn and weep. But soon I shall go to see the girl once more. Meantime and all time heaven bless her! I can do nothing without Lydia—not even read.²³

Parker was ordained to the Unitarian ministry and installed as the pastor of the West Roxbury Church on June 21, 1837. People who had been, and continued to be, important in Parker's life were in attendance at the ordination-installation service. Some New England notables were there. The aged John Quincy Adams—upon whose future death Parker would deliver a memorable memorial address—came up from Quincy. Dr. Convers Francis, who had been so helpful and influential in Parker's pre-seminary days, delivered the ordination sermon. He challenged the candidate not to neglect his studies. Henry Ware, who had contributed so much to the development of Parker's oratorical skills, offered the ordaining prayer, asking the Almighty that Parker's fondness for learning might not keep him from God's work. Caleb Stetson delivered the charge, and George Ripley of Brook Farm, along with others, extended the right hand of fellowship. John Dwight and John Pierpont each furnished a hymn. It was a solemn and impressive ceremony, a memorable moment in a life that would have many memorable moments.

It was during his years at West Roxbury that Parker came under the influence of Transcendentalism, a philosophy "prone to find deep religious meanings in all created things." This New England movement had its first stirring as early as 1820, but it was not until 1836 that it began to take a definite form. That was the year Emerson published his manifesto of Transcendentalism, *Nature*, and Orestes Bronson wrote his social critique, *New Views of Christianity, Society and the Church*. Parker's attendance at Transcendental meetings began in 1837 when he was one of the youngest members of that sophisticated and intellectually renowned circle. The roll call of names belonging to that group—some more involved than others—constitutes a Hall of Fame in United States intellectual, cultural, and reform history: Bronson Alcott, John Allen, Charles Bradford, Orestes Bronson, William Ellery Channing, Christopher Cranch, Charles Dana, John Dwight, Ralph Waldo Emerson, Margaret Fuller,

Nathaniel Hawthorne, Isaac Heckler, Charles Newcomb, Elizabeth and Sophia Peabody, George Ripley, Henry David Thoreau, and many others. It was Emerson's famous Divinity School address to the graduating class in the summer of 1838 that especially inspired and motivated Parker in the Transcendental faith. Writing to a friend, Parker described his reaction to Emerson's words. "So beautiful, so just, so true, and terribly sublime was his picture of the faults of the Church in its present position. My soul is roused, and this week I shall write the long-meditated sermon on the state of the Church and the duties of these times."[24]

Soon after establishing his ministry at West Roxbury, Parker would walk over to George Ripley's Brook Farm two or three times a week, and every Sunday there would be a delegation from Brook Farm in Parker's congregation. Many members of the Transcendental Club were Unitarian clergymen who were protesting against the more conservative theological and social assumptions of the "Boston Unitarians." Some of these clergymen—Emerson, Allen, Dwight, Ripley—eventually left the ministry and the church, considering the institution to be unredeemable. Most, however, like Parker, chose to remain within the church and seek reform from the inside. "Eleven of the seventeen clergymen in the original Transcendental group remained all their lives in the ministerial profession, and . . . all but two of the seventeen had ministerial careers lasting ten years or more."[25]

Broadly interpreted, Transcendentalism was an American expression of Romanticism, stressing a return to idealism over the sensism of the Enlightenment. The Transcendentalists looked to Plato and Kant for inspiration rather than John Locke as did those who represented the Enlightenment. Within these rather wide parameters each Transcendentalist formulated his own unique outlook. About 1850, Parker was ready to express his interpretation of the movement. In an article that was not published until ten years after his death, Parker began by differentiating between two types of knowing (metaphysics). There was, first of all, the "sensational school," which declared, "there is nothing in the intellect which was not first in the senses." This was the metaphysics of the Enlightenment, of induction and empiricism. "The senses are the windows which let in all the light I have. . . . I reflect upon this, and by reflection transform a sensation into an idea. An idea therefore, is a transformed sensation."[26]

There was another means of knowing, however, a higher and better way, the transcendental way.

There is in the intellect (or consciousness), something that never was in the senses, to wit, the intellect (or consciousness) itself; that man has faculties which transcend the senses; faculties which give him ideas and intuitions that transcend sensational experience; ideas whose origin is not from sensation, nor their proof from sensation. This is the transcendental school.[27]

The source of ethics, then, is to be found in a person's own "moral faculties which leads him to justice and right, and by his own nature can find out what is right and just, and can know it and be certain of it." This is the "higher law" that Parker would so often refer to in his later fight to abolish slavery and other social wrongs. Sometimes he called this inner moral faculty "conscience," which was in all moral matters "complete and reliable. Conscience shows what should be and shall."

To know what is right, I need not ask what is the current practice, what say the Revised Statutes, what said holy men of old, but what says the conscience? what, God? The common practice, the Revised Statutes, the holy men of old, are helps, not masters. I am to be co-ordinate with justice.[28]

Religion, as ethics, also had its truest source in consciousness, the intuition of humankind.

Now the transcendental philosophy legitimates the ideas of religion by reference to human nature. Some of them it finds truths of necessity, which cannot be conceived of as false or unreal without violence to reason; some it finds are truths of consciousness,—of spontaneous consciousness, or demonstration, inductive or deductive. Such ideas, capable of this legitimation, transcend experience, require and admit no further proof; as true before experience as after; true before time, after time, eternally; absolutely true.[29]

Experience and observation, therefore, are not the sources of religion, but can be helpful in verifying and illustrating that which is intuitional.

[Religion] does not neglect experience. In human history it finds confirmations, illustrations, of the ideas of human nature, for history represents the attempt of mankind to develop human nature. So then as transcendentalism in philosophy legitimates religion by a reference to truths of necessity, to truths of consciousness, it illustrates religion by facts of observation, facts of testimony.[30]

Transcendentalism was, according to Parker, a new way of perceiving truth, morals, and religion. Conscience, higher or inner law, reason, intuition—call it what you will—was to be the guiding light. There was a task to be accomplished, reforms to be made in all walks of life, and Parker was confident that this new way would lead to a promising and better future.

The problem of transcendental philosophy is no less than this, to revise the experience of mankind; to test ethics by conscience, science by reason; to try the creeds of the churches, the constitutions of the states by the constitution of the universe; to reverse what is wrong, supply what is wanting, and command the just. . . . It has little of history behind, for this philosophy is young. It looks to a future, a future to be made; a church whose creed is truth, whose worship love; a society full of industry and abundance, full of wisdom, virtue, and the poetry of life; a state with unity among all, with freedom for each; a church without tyranny, a society without ignorance, want, or crime, a state without oppression; yes, a world with no war among the nations to consume the work of their hands, and no restrictive policy to hinder the welfare of mankind. That is the human dream of the transcendental philosophy. Shall it ever become a fact? History says, No; human nature says, Yes.[31]

These would be the ideas that would dominate Parker's words and actions for the rest of his days. Perry Miller has noted Parker's influence upon the Transcendental movement, declaring that Parker was "next only to Emerson—and in the world of action even above Emerson—to give shape and meaning to the Transcendental movement in America."[32] In September of 1850—the same year the above thoughts were written—Parker delivered a sermon, titled, "The Function and Place of Conscience in Relation to the Laws of Man," which was a reaffirmation of these transcendental ideas.

So there are likewise certain constant and general facts which occur in what may be called the spiritual world, the world of internal consciousness. They represent the laws of spirit—that is, of the human spirit—in virtue of which things are designed to take place so and not otherwise. These laws are the same everywhere and always; they never change. They are not made by men, but only discovered by men. They are inherent in the constitution of man. . . . They seem designed to secure the welfare of the spiritual world. They represent the infinity of God in the world of man, His infinite power, wisdom, justice, love and holiness. . . . [These] laws . . . depend for their execution only on the infinite will of God, and so cannot be violated. The laws of man depend for their execution also on the finite will of man, and so may be broken.[33]

Unitarianism had come about because some New England Congregationalists wished to travel what some thought were radically new theological paths. The movement became a certified denomination in 1825 when the American Unitarian Association (AUA) was formed in Boston with 125 churches under its new banner. Prior to this those with Unitarian leanings were looked upon as the liberal wing of New England Congregationalism. The "representative man" of this newly formed denomination was William Ellery Channing, pastor of the Federal Street Church in Boston. In an 1830 address, Channing sought to stake out the new and broad dimensions of American Unitarianism.

It seems to me of singular importance that Christianity should be recognized and presented in its true character, as I have aimed to place it before you this day. The low views of religion, which have prevailed too long, should give place to this highest one. They suited perhaps darker ages. But they have done their work, and should pass away. Christianity should now be disencumbered and set free. . . . It should come forth from the darkness and corruption of the past in its own celestial splendor, and in it divine simplicity. It should be comprehended as having but one purpose, the perfection of human nature, the elevation of men into nobler beings.[34]

It was not long before divisions began to trouble the new denomination. Debate arose over how much tradition "should pass away," and how much needed to be preserved so that Unitarianism could still be defined and accepted as Christian. The Transcendental Unitarians wanted a radical break with the past. As has been noted, there were those who dismissed the institutional church as no longer relevant and separated from it. Other Transcendental Unitarians—the majority it would seem—followed the examples of Channing and Parker and remained within the church. The debate—often bitter and acrimonious as theological and religious differences so often tend to be—would continue for several years. In an 1853 statement of faith, the AUA—sometimes referred to as the Boston Unitarians—reaffirmed its supernatural faith, seeking to disassociate itself from the more radical elements of the denomination.

We desire openly to declare our belief as a denomination, so far as it can be officially represented by the American Unitarian Association, that God, moved by his own love, did raise up Jesus to aid in our redemption from sin, did by him pour a fresh flood of purifying life through the withered veins of humanity and along the corrupted channels of the world, and is, by his religion, forever sweeping the nations with regenerating gales from heaven, and visiting the hearts of men with celestial solicitations. We receive the teachings of Christ, separated from all foreign admixtures and later accretions, as infallible truth from God.[35]

Channing was an important part of Parker's education into liberalism, and the student would eventually outdistance the teacher. During his first five years at West Roxbury, the young minister would often meet with the older Channing, and the two intellectuals would exchange thoughts on philosophy, history, theology, and other weighty topics. Parker came to fully accept Channing's basic premise: "The truth is that our ultimate reliance is and must be on our own reason. I am surer that my rational nature is from God than that any book is an expression of his will." The two did not always agree. Parker thought that Channing's acceptance of miracles, though not the Scriptures, was an inconsistency. Channing thought that Parker was too harsh in his criticisms of the church. They differed over the merits of various Revolutionary Fathers—Channing championed Sam Adams, Parker thought Jefferson the best. The two men differed in temperament; Parker could be intemperate and uncompromising, whereas Channing possessed a much more gentle and accepting nature. Channing attempted to avoid controversy, Parker seemed to seek it, even revel in it. Nevertheless, the two men were kindred spirits and mutually admired each other. Parker said, "I felt there was a broad common ground between us."[36] When Parker heard of Channing's death on October 2, 1842, he wrote to a friend: "You know, as all do, that no man in America has done so much to promote truth, virtue and religion as he. I feel that I have lost one of the most valuable friends I ever had. His mind was wide and his heart was wider yet." In his journal, Parker noted: "No man since Washington has done so much to elevate his country."[37] Parker wondered why it was that Channing had died and not himself. "Few would mourn my departure," he lamented. "Why am I spared?" The mantle of liberal leadership, Parker sensed, had now fallen on him. "Let me but finish the work now in my hands."[38]

WEST ROXBURY SERMONS

Before assuming the pastorate at West Roxbury in 1837, Parker had written about forty sermons, some of which had been delivered before his peers at the Divinity School, others at various churches in the interim before assuming duties at his first charge. In his *Experience As A Minister*, Parker recalled those early sermons.

Of course, my first sermons were only imitations; and even if the thought might perhaps be original, the form was old, the stereotype of the pulpit. I preached with fear and trembling, and wondered that old and mature persons, rich in the experiences of life, should listen to a young man, who might indeed have read and thought, but yet had no time to live much and know things by heart. I took all possible pains with the matter of the discourse, and always appealed to the religious instincts of mankind. At the beginning I resolved to preach the natural laws of man as they are writ in his constitution, no less and no more. After preaching a few months in various places, and feeling my way into the consciousness of man, I determined to preach nothing as religion which I had not experienced inwardly and made my own, knowing it by heart. Thus not only the intellectual, but also the religious part of my sermons would rest on facts that I was sure of, and not on the word of another.[39]

During his nine years at West Roxbury, Parker delivered 362 different sermons to the congregation. He kept a careful record of his preaching, and it is known that some of these sermons were repeated several times. One sermon was preached twenty-five times; others as often as ten or twelve times. There was a wide range between the levels of learning in that congregation, and Parker was able to deliver sermons that met the variety of needs, interests, and understanding among those who heard him. One sermon was titled, "The Temptations of Milkmen."[40] In *Experience As A Minister*, Parker spoke of the congregation at West Roxbury, "one of the smallest societies in New England, where I found men and women whose friendship is still dear and instructive." He knew the people well and worked hard on sermons that would address their concerns.

For the first year or two the congregation did not exceed seventy persons, including the children. I soon became well acquainted with all in the little parish, where I found some men of rare enlightenment, some truly generous and noble souls. I knew the characters of all, and the thoughts of such as had them. I took great pains with the composition of my sermons; they were never out of my mind. I had an intense delight in writing and preaching; but I was a learner quite as much as a teacher, and was feeling my way forward and upward with one hand, while I tried to lead men with the other. I preached natural laws, nothing on the authority of any church, any tradition, any sect, though I sought illustration and confirmation in all these sources. For historical things I told the historical evidence; for spiritual things I found ready proof in the primal instincts of the soul, and confirmation in the life of religious men. The simple life of the farmers, mechanics, and milkmen about me, of its own accord, turned into a sort of poetry, and reappeared in the sermons, as the green woods not far off looked in at the windows of the meeting-house. I think I preached only what I had experienced in my own inward consciousness, which widened and grew richer as I came into piratical contact with living men, turned time into life, and mere thought became character.[41]

In 1892 Samuel J. Barrows edited a volume of fifteen Parker sermons delivered at West Roxbury, many of which Parker had delivered a number of times. Thus, Barrows seemed to be choosing those sermons that Parker himself, by repetition, felt to be the most important. The sermons are placed in the book, *West Roxbury Sermons*, in chronological order, and it is possible to perceive a progression of thought taking place over the years, from the simple to the more complex, from less controversial to more controversial themes. These are not the well-known sermons of the middle and latter years of his ministry, but are important for the very reason that they do represent the beginning. An 1837 sermon, "The Parable of the Talents," represented a theme that could safely be delivered from almost any pulpit.

The idea which this parable was designed to set forth is this: that a man's happiness on earth and in heaven depends solely upon the use he makes of his powers. Various faculties and different opportunities are afforded to different men; but a man's merit and virtue consist entirely in the use he makes of them. Thus he who receives two talents and gains two is not less meritorious than he who receives five and gains other five, nor is the reward the less. It is the use, not the amount, of talents that constitutes virtue and of course happiness; for virtue is the immediate cause of happiness.[42]

In the same year, "Spiritual Indifference" was another sermon with a theme that ministers have been emphasizing for centuries.

It is sadly the truth that saving here and there a sainted few, Christianity made for man, sent down by God for his blessing, does not bring forth half of its just fruits. There is enough of sanctimonious looks, enough attention perhaps to the appearance and form of godliness, but where is its power and spirit? There are listeners in churches, eloquent voices proclaiming truth; but does religion go to the market-place, the workshop, the fireside and fieldside? Does it mingle in our every-day concerns? Is it made real as life? An ancient philosopher lighted a lamp by day, and in the streets of a populous city sought for a man, a complete, true man; but he did not find one. Should he make the experiment now, and look for that true man, who is the only true Christian, would he find one? Would it be you or I? Why not?[43]

A third sermon from that first year at West Roxbury was on "Tranquility," a sermon that could be adopted by many contemporary "positive-thinker" preachers. One wonders how well Parker was able to apply this virtue to himself, especially only a few years later when he would always be at the center of some controversy. The first two or three years at West Roxbury were indeed, by Parker's own admission, tranquil, the best of years. It would soon change. But in 1837, Parker experienced—as much as it was possible for Theodore Parker to do so—and could preach about the importance of tranquility.

Amid many virtues never before called out there is one crying fault which shows itself everywhere. . . . This fault is restlessness, a want of calmness and tranquility. It belongs eminently to our times. . . . Great men are the calmest of all the children of humanity. . . . We shall find that all of these high spirits have been men of tranquility,—never noisy, obtrusive, impetuous, fearful lest their name be forgotten; for they cared not for self, not trembling lest the great cause of truth in their hands should come to an untimely end, for they knew it was God's cause, and would prevail. . . . Haste, violence, are utterly opposed to the calm, noiseless spirit of religion. . . . In all religious exercises, when piety with open face looks up to God, and when in the stillness of solitude thou art alone with God, let there be calmness.[44]

The following year, 1838, the West Roxbury preacher delivered a sermon, "The World Belongs to Each Man." In this sermon Parker used the homey touch, skillfully and poetically drawing illustrations from nature and everyday life—a rhetorical technique he so often used.

He who is a true and sound man in the city rejoices at the bales of goods he sees in the streets, in the great ships that bring us the fruits of other lands, in the wealth of the warehouses, in the splendor of the buildings, without dreaming of the ownership. In the country; he may admire the beautiful landscape before him,—the cattle in the field, the trees in the orchard, the brooks in the meadows, the farmhouse which man has built, the flowers and corn he has planted,—asking no question as to the legal owners thereof. He may say, All these are mine. . . . The rose in the garden wafts its fragrance to the boy in the street; it is as grateful to him as to the man in whose garden it grows. . . . The breath of morn, the rising sweet with song of earliest bird, the crimson twilight, are his, and he enjoys them. The strength of noonday is his. The sober majesty of evening, the awful solemnity of night, all are his.[45]

In 1840 a different kind of sermon began to emerge. In "The Application of Religion to Life," Parker talks about the relationship of religion to various social reform movements that are beginning to arise in America, most especially in New England. These were matters more marked by controversy, many in which Parker himself would become much involved. The sermon strikes a much different tone and temperament than the sermons of 1837.

There are three ways in which religion may be applied to life,—individually, socially, and politically. . . . It may be taken for granted that attempts are very rarely made to make a political application of Christianity to life. . . .

Again, extensive attempts are not made to apply religion to live socially, though perhaps we do more in this respect than other nations. We are so accustomed to its evils that we do not think of them. We do not look on almshouses and asylums, and ask how men are become poor in a civilized land, in a Christian land, while more suffer from want than among savages. We do not look on our jails and ask why its inmates are there, and what circumstances forced them to crime. We do not look on the fact that seventeen men out of the score have the fear of poverty before them all their life, while God made enough and to spare for the whole world. We do not consider that three fourths of men and women, as things now are, toil of necessity so large a portion of their time that nothing is left for improvement,—absolutely nothing for intellectual improvement. . . . This is . . . the earthly end of religion,—to make this world a better place, to cast out the devils from it. . . . Yet it is commonly thought religion is only for the next life. . . . Religion makes heaven here. . . .

We see in our day various attempts to apply Christianity to life. Temperance societies . . . Abolition societies . . . peace and non-resistance societies. . . . These societies are numerous, and certainly constitute one of the most pleasing and promising signs of the times. They show that religion is coming out of the Church, and girding herself for the world of work that lies before her. These efforts are good; they are noble and divine. . . . But now, when Christianity nods over her Bible, and sleeps in her pew of a Sunday, while she makes slaves or keeps them, and strives to render the rich richer and the poor poorer all the week, the world cannot afford to be nice, and criticize the only men that are awake and striving to do the world service. . . .

You cannot be individually a Christian and socially a heathen and politically a savage.[46]

In 1841 there was a discourse entitled, "A Sermon of Man." In this sermon, for the first time, Parker divided the nature of man into four parts: "the understanding, the affections, and the moral and religious sentiments." It was a division to which Parker would often return in the years to come. Each part contained an element of the divine, and because of this the potentialities and possibilities of humankind were limitless.[47]

In an 1844 sermon on "Christian Advancement," Parker challenged his listeners to continual growth in every aspect of their lives. Though growth was a natural phenomena, it could be impeded or even stopped when a person believed that he or she had attained all. To illustrate his point that growth and development are an ongoing process, the preacher spoke of an evolutionary process in nature, an insight Parker proclaimed some sixteen years before Darwin's *Origin of Species.*

In the visible world there is what philosophy calls a law of continuity. All is done gradually, nothing by leaps. Invisibly the vegetable and animal world approach and intermingle. You cannot tell where the mineral kingdom begins, and the animal ends. They must be distinguished by their center, not their circumference; by a type, not a limit. There are visible links that connect beast and bird, fish and insect. In animals lower down you see hints that a man is yet to be. In man you see as it were vestiges of the lower animals, a certain bruteness which it is difficult to explain, perhaps more difficult to manage. This brute element sometimes astonishes you in yourself.[48]

"God's Income in Man" was first preached in 1846. Parker once more pressed his theme of the divine in man and all of nature. "All things have their ultimate ground in God. He is their life, their being, the source of all this river of beauty, this lake of fire, this ocean of existence." Yet, Parker was becoming increasingly aware that many people failed to discover, deliberately ignored, or openly defied the divine within. In this sermon, as he will often do in later sermons, Parker depicts foreboding images of those who have misused their lives.

Others by selfishness, by an exclusive counselling with prudence or worldly thrift, by a sluggish refusal even to look up to the great Source of righteousness and truth and good, turn away from their proper actions and lose the power of right,—men of low aims, content with one good action in their life, content with seeming good, content with appearances, not seeking perfection; men that sell themselves to things as they are, instead of giving themselves away to truth and righteousness, to goodness and to God. The world is full of such men,—men who cease to grow, who are content to belittle, who despair of heroism in themselves, and mock at brave endeavors in all other men, calling that madness or fanaticism. Men that are mired in worldliness are subdued to that they wallow in. . . .

I have seen a man with large powers, exceeding great, but proud, rebellious, violent, and self-willed,—a sneaky-minded man, forever in a coil, or moving with a wriggling gait from thought to thought. ,. . . and so the man grows less and less, and like that ancient worm crawls with prone face and feeds upon the dust, counting it life to shed a poison glitter in the sun, and with discordant thrust to hiss at the passers-by, or lurking in the grass, with calumnious tooth to bite a good man's heel.[49]

West Roxbury Sermons closed with an 1848 sermon, "The Doctrine of Inspiration." The sermon begins by stating that divine inspiration is often thought of as something received by a very few people and in the long ago. Such a view, Parker retorts, "is erroneous and full of danger," based upon "a false theology . . . a false view of man . . . a false view of God." God, according to Parker, still inspires those who are open to his promptings. "Whence come the ideas of eternity, truth, right, love of God? From myself? Not at all. I am finite; they infinite. From men? They also are finite. Nay, from God himself."

Let me take one form of inspiration, the intellectual. When I receive truth, I receive the thought of God; when I receive this from another, I receive the thought of God indirectly and am indirectly inspired,—inspired through the medium of another mind. When I discover the truth myself, then I receive it straightway from God, then, I am inspired directly, immediately.

This was the Transcendental idea that became the core of Parker's theology. God speaks directly to man, here and now, through reason, conscience and intuition. People today can receive a revelation from God just as surely as did the prophets and apostles of old. "There are various degrees of inspiration," noted Parker, "from Christ down to the humblest man, the wickedest sinner. No man is wholly without it." The preacher concluded that "the first thing in the counsel of God must ever be to impart his spirit to all his sons."[50]

The sermons at West Roxbury represent the early Parker, those years before he moved to Boston where be gained international fame as "the great American preacher." The West Roxbury sermons are important, nevertheless, for they demonstrate a progression of thought and manner in the young preacher. The earliest sermons in that small parish were safe, non-controversial in nature; but as the years went by, Parker became bolder, more confident, and more willing to take on the controversial in his rhetorical utterances.

It was in West Roxbury that Parker developed oratorical habits that he would never forsake. Though Parker's sermons and lectures were always scholarly and read from a manuscript, they were delivered with a passion and an emotion that sometimes hid the depth of his words. Parker's formal manner did not fail to excite his listeners, for he not only believed in superior ideas, but also in the superiority of sentiment, passion and emotions. Though a man of great learning and an impressive vocabulary, Parker was always careful to deliver his messages in ideas and words that his audience could understand. Rufus Leighton, who has made an extensive study of the words and writings of Parker, has commented: "Although he was one of the giants of learning, his style is remarkable for its freedom from all taint of scholastic and metaphysical terms."[51] John White Chadwick has written of the "homeliness" of Parker's vocabulary.

Of the homeliness [of] his vocabulary [there] was sufficient proof. Ninety-one of his words out of each hundred were Anglo-Saxon, to eighty-five of Webster's and seventy-four of Sumner's. Counting incidently one of his pages, I was astonished at the number of words and found I had been counting monosyllables for the most part.[52]

Parker's practice of delivering scholarly discourses in a manner that most people could understand began early in his ministry. The parishioners at his first charge in West Roxbury were ordinary people—farmers, mechanics, small merchants, and milkmen—and the young minister knew how important it was for these people to understand him. He purposed "to preach nothing as religion that I have not experienced inwardly and made my own." In an 1838 letter to William Silsbe, Parker wrote: "I feel bound to communicate my views just so fast and so far as men can understand them,—no farther. If they do not understand them when I propose them, the fault, I think, is mine, and not theirs."[53]

When Parker moved on to Boston where he spoke to much larger and more sophisticated audiences, his brilliance was still communicated through a certain simplicity. A laborer who came to hear Parker, afterward exclaimed: "Is that Theodore Parker? You told me he was a remarkable man; but I understood every word he said."[54] Parker wrote of his efforts to use "plain, simple words."

In my preaching I have used plain, simple words. . . . and counted nothing unclean, because merely common. . . . I have always preferred to use, when fit, the every-day words in which men think and talk, scold, make love, and pray, so that generous-hearted philosophy, clad in common dress, might more easily become familiar to plaid-clad men. It is with customary tools that we work easiest and best. . . . I have . . . on my side, the examples of all the great masters of speech . . . Homer, Dante, Shakespeare . . . Luther, Latimer, Barrows, and South.[55]

3

The Years of Influence (1841–1859)

Theodore Parker never wrote a formal pamphlet or book on rhetoric or homiletics. He never had the opportunity to deliver the Yale Lectures on Preaching as did Henry Ward Beecher (three times) and Phillips Brooks, for Parker died several years before the Yale Lectures were inaugurated. Nevertheless, from his own sermons and lectures, from thoughts recorded in his *Journal*, from letters he wrote, and from the testimonies of those who heard him, it is possible to construct a tower of information on the rhetorical techniques that made Parker one of the most memorable of orators in a time saturated with great oratory.

If a person was to be a speaker who was "permanently impressive," Parker emphasized, "he must be a person of superior ideas."[1] Such ideas were the greatest of all human forces. Parker himself was the embodiment of "superior ideas." He was endowed with an intellect of the highest rank, having read Homer and Plutarch before he was eight; the poets Pope, Milton, Cowley, and Dryden before he was ten. By the time of his mid-thirties, Parker had mastered twenty languages. He may have possessed the greatest intellect ever to grace the American pulpit. Taking into account such intellectual clerics as the Mathers, Jonathan Edwards, and William Ellery Channing, Parker's mind would still seem to be unsurpassed. He nourished this great intellect by voracious reading over a wide diversity of subjects. His list of books read for the year 1836 alone numbered 320 volumes. Chadwick has written of Parker that "knowledge of all kinds had for him an irresistible attraction." When Parker was in Europe in 1843, he met the noted scholar, F. C. Baur, at Tubingen. When Parker asked Baur how many hours a day he studied, the German professor replied, "Alas! only eighteen." Parker noted that was two to three hours more than the maximum he had allowed himself.[2] By the time of his death the volumes in his library numbered 20,000, a library that Commager has written was the "richest and most varied library in the whole of New England."³ That library is now located in a special section of the Boston Public Library to which Parker willed it should go. That Parker designated a public library rather than a university library to be the recipient of his books is significant. The preacher desired that his volumes would be available to people from all walks of life, not just the academic elites. McCall describes the appearance and contents of Parker's library. "Upon the dusty shelves are books in thirty languages; books of history, literature, theology, philosophy, logic, mathematics, zoology, chemistry, physics, law, biography; books rare and ancient, books that were modern in his day; books of all the great masters. Practically all of them show evidence of use, though few are annotated."⁴

There were acquaintances who suggested to Parker that maybe he studied too much. At Parker's ordination service, the Reverend Henry Ware Jr., who had been Parker's rhetorical mentor at the Divinity School, prayed that Parker's fondness for the pursuit of knowledge might not divert him from accomplishing God's work.⁵ Parker's friend, John Dwight, once wrote to Parker: "I think your love of learning is a passion, that it injures your mind by converting insensibly what is originally a pure thirst for truth into a greedy, avaricious, jealous striving, not merely to know but to get all there is to be known."⁶ Ware and Dwight, along with several others, need not have worried that too much learning would spoil Parker's effectiveness. Parker did indeed spend much time in the pursuit and development of "superior ideas." However, he was able to transform "superior ideas" into rhetorical forms that inspired and motivated multitudes, even people with limited educations.

Parker's great learning was widely recognized. As early as 1842, the *Richmond Examiner* (Virginia) observed: "This man commands at every touch the literature of the world."⁷ Four years later the *Streeter's Weekly Boston Star* acknowledged: "It is thought, by those competent to judge, that over and above his theological learning, Mr. Parker—although now but thirty-six years of age—has a more extensive general knowledge than any other man living, except it may be Lord Broughham."⁸

Parker reflected deeply on those things he read, observed and experienced. After the gathering of information, reflection was an essential component in his preparation. In a letter to his friend Keach, he wrote: "It is a good thing before writing anything, to think over the subject and see what you know about it, then to make a plan of your work."⁹ He used much of his traveling time for reflection. "I did not abandon my scholarly work while traveling and lecturing," Parker noted. "The motion of the railroad cars gave a pleasing and not harmful stimulus to thought."¹⁰ In a letter to Miss Glover, Parker emphasized that reflection must precede writing. "I have no receipt for writing," he observed, "except to think the subject all over long before writing—then to think over the form of the thing, arrange the parts, and see if they are well proportioned, and make up a whole. Then I write."¹¹

Parker had a talent for remembering what he read and observed, and an even greater talent for organizing those amassed facts into a coherent order. James Freeman Clark, a contemporary of Parker, noted: "His [Parker's] memory of details was astounding; but his power of systematizing those details—making them drill in companies, and march in squadrons, and take on the order of battle—was equally striking."[12] Organization was paramount for Parker. It was not enough for the accomplished speaker to have good ideas, even "superior ideas." He must be able to organize and arrange those ideas in an orderly and carefully constructed fashion. Parker criticized some of the most eminent orators of his day for their carelessness when it came to organization. He said that Emerson lacked "the power of orderly arrangement to a remarkable degree. . . . his deep sayings are jewels strung wholly at random."[13] He complained that Channing's "arrangement is frequently unphilosophical,"[14] and that John Quincy Adams's "productions are disorderly."[15] In May 1858, Parker wrote an article about Henry Ward Beecher in *Atlantic Monthly*. Most of the article was full of praise for the Brooklyn preacher, but his one criticism was that Beecher failed to "put ultimate facts in a row."[16] Roy C. McCall, a scholar of rhetoric, has summarized Parker's organizational skills.

As models of clear and logical outline, Parker's sermons are scarcely excelled. Whatever may be said of the other qualities of his composition, his organization is adequate. Some might criticize it for its sameness of "stating the proposition and then proving it" and for its invariable adherence of the fourfold method of introduction, thesis, discussion, and conclusion; but as a means of fundamental exposition that aims at persuasion as the remote end, this traditional outline probably will not soon be improved.[17]

Throughout a sermon or lecture Parker would often amass great amounts of information to support his thesis. It was imperative for him to be accurate in the presentation of such great quantities of data. He was not a person who would tolerate carelessness in presentations. In an 1849 sermon, Parker spoke of "The Moral Condition of Boston." He laid out many facts and numbers to demonstrate his theme that Boston was an immoral city. Furthermore, he wanted his audience to know he was not exaggerating. "Let me speak soberly," he said, "exaggeration is a figure of speech I would always banish from my rhetoric, here, above all, where the fact is more appalling than any fancy I could invent."[18]

Each address followed a logical sequence of ideas, much as a lawyer would present his brief in a court of law. Parker began the preparation of his orations with an outline to which he faithfully adhered as he wrote out his sermon or lecture. Such a procedure kept his material organized. The process was almost always the same. In the introduction he presented his theme or proposition. "This proposition he invariably stated openly, frankly, clearly, thus conforming to the first Aristotelian requirement and to the homiletical advice of the period."[19] During the main body of the discourse, the theme or proposition was further defined, supported and proved. Parker concluded, as was commonly done in that era, by calling upon his listeners to respond in some way to what they had heard.

Peter Dean, a nineteenth-century biographer of Parker, has written that Parker "generally wrote his sermons at the beginning of the week, and left a page or two for thoughts to be written on Saturday night."[20] Once Parker began to write, he wrote rapidly and seldom revised what he had written. In a letter to Elizabeth Peabody, in January of 1841, the preacher revealed: "I write swiftly though I think slowly, and so many of the literary defects of all my writing are no doubt the result of haste."[21] His lengthy oration on Daniel Webster is an example. Of it, Parker wrote in his journal: "At eleven o'clock Wednesday night not a line of it was written; at two p.m. Saturday not a line unwritten."[22]

In delivering his orations, Parker read from his carefully prepared manuscript. There was, nevertheless, an impromptu quality in his speeches. McCall has written:

Parker was unquestionably a manuscript preacher. This fact does not mean, however, that his preaching was devoid of extempore quality. In his early preaching, he delivered the written word, but added much that was better and more reaching extemporaneously. In latter years the practice was to write more than he had time to preach and to omit portions at the time of delivery. He invariably read from the manuscript, but his dependence there on was not so complete as to rob his speech of extempore freshness and audience adaptation.[23]

During the middle and latter years of his career—the years of influence (1841–1859)—there were at least three major areas upon which Theodore Parker focused his oratorical attention: (1) theological and ecclesiastical reform, (2) social reform, and (3) biographical topics.

THEOLOGICAL AND ECCLESIASTICAL REFORM

"A Discourse On The Transient And Permanent In Christianity"[24] (1841)

On May 19, 1841, Parker delivered the sermon at the ordination of Charles C. Shackford at the Hawes Place Church in Boston. Though there had been rumors and suspicions of Parker's unorthodoxy before this date, it was this sermon, more than anything else, that drew attention to Parker's deviation from popularly accepted theology. Entitled, "A Discourse on the Transient and Permanent in Christianity," the sermon attempted to set forth what Parker believed to be eternally true in religion and that which, though popular dogma, was merely passing.

Looking at the Word of Jesus, at real Christianity, the pure religion he taught, nothing appears more fixed and certain. . . . While true religion is always the same thing, in each century and every land, in each man that feels it, the Christianity of the pulpit, which is the religion taught, the Christianity of the people, which is the religion that is accepted and lived out, has never been the same thing in any two centuries or lands, except only in name.

Unfortunately, noted Parker, more attention

is generally given to the transient in Christianity than to the permanent therein. It must be confessed, though with sorrow, that transient things form a great part of what is commonly taught as religion. An undue place has often been assigned to forms and doctrines, while too little stress has been laid on the divine life of the soul, love to God, and love to man. . . .

While this [true] religion is one and always the same thing, there may be numerous systems of theology or philosophies of religion. . . . So the Christianity of Jesus is permanent, though what passes for Christianity with popes and catechisms, with sects and churches, in the first century or in the nineteenth century, prove transient.

Parker continued to press the argument that all theological doctrines are transitory.

Any one, who traces the history of what is called Christianity, will see that nothing changes more from age to age than the doctrines taught as Christian, and insisted on as essential to Christianity and personal salvation. What is falsehood in one province passes for truth in another. The heresy of one age is the orthodox belief and "only infallible rule" of the next. . . . Men are burned for professing what men are burned for denying. . . . The stream of Christianity, as men receive it, has caught a stain from every soil it has filtered through, so that now it is not the pure water from the well of life, which is offered to our lips, but streams troubled and polluted by man with mire and dirt. If Paul and Jesus could read our books of theological doctrines, would they accept as their teaching what men have invented in their name? . . . Therefore, our theological doctrines, are imperfect, and so perishing.

How does one know that which is permanent or that which is transient in religion? Here, Parker returns to an idea he internalized early in his life. True religion, permanent religion, is known by intuition or instinct. "If we are faithful," Parker asserted, "the great truths of morality and religion, the deep sentiment of love to man and love to God, are perceived intuitively, and by instinct, as it were, though our theology be imperfect and miserable."

Parker then singled out two specific doctrines that have been treated and believed as eternally true, but are in reality impermanent and fading. The first had to do with the doctrine of biblical inerrancy, the idea that the Bible must be without error or inconsistencies. He began by pointing to the Old Testament.

He was deemed no small sinner who found mistakes in the manuscripts. On the authority of the written word man was taught to believe impossible legends, conflicting assertions; to take fiction for fact; a dream for a miraculous revelation of God; an oriental poem for a grave history of miraculous events; a collection of amatory idyls for a serious discourse "touching the mutual love of Christ and the Church;" they have been taught to accept a picture sketched by some glowing eastern imagination, never intended to be taken for a reality, as a proof that the Infinite God spoke in human words, appeared in the shape of a cloud, a flaming bush, or a man who ate, and drank, and vanished into smoke; that he gave counsels to-day, and the opposite to-morrow; that he violated his own laws; was angry, and was only dissuaded by a mortal man from destroying at once a whole nation—millions of men who rebelled against their leader in a moment of anguish. Questions in philosophy, questions in the Christian religion, have been settled by an appeal to that book. The inspiration of its authors has been assumed as infallible. Every fact in the early Jewish history has been taken as a type of some analogous fact in Christian history. The most distant events, even such as are still in the arena of time, were supposed to be clearly foreseen and foretold by pious Hebrews several centuries before Christ. It has been assumed at the outset, with no shadow of evidence, that those writers held a miraculous communication with God, such as he has granted to no other man.

Parker attested, "this idolatry of the Old Testament has not always existed." In the present, "modern criticism is fast breaking to pieces this idol which men have made out of the scriptures." He then turned his attention to the New Testament.

The history of opinions on the New Testament is quite similar. It has been assumed at the outset, it would seem with no sufficient reason, without the smallest pretense on its writers' part, that all of its authors were infallibly and miraculously inspired, so that they could commit no error of doctrine or fact. Men have been bid to close their eyes at the obvious differences between Luke and John—the serious disagreement between Paul and Peter; to believe, on the smallest evidence, accounts which shock the moral sense and revolt the reason.

Parker assured that "the current notions respecting the infallible inspiration of the Bible have no foundation in the Bible itself." He asked: "Which Evangelist, which Apostle of the New Testament, what Prophet or Psalmist of the Old Testament, ever claims infallible authority for himself or for others? . . . Would not those modest writers themselves be confounded at the idolatry we pay them?"

A second doctrine that people believed to be a permanent truth, when in fact it was transient, had to do with the nature and authority of Christ. Parker reviewed what he perceived to be the confusion on this matter.

Another instance of the transitoriness of doctrines, taught as Christian, is found in those which relate to the nature and authority of Christ. One ancient party has told us, that he is the infinite God; another, that he is both God and man; a third, that he was a man, the son of Joseph and Mary,—born as we are; tempted like ourselves; inspired, as we may be, if we pay the price. Each of the former parties believed its doctrine on this head was infallibly true, and formed the very substance of Christianity, and was one of the essential conditions of salvation, though scarce any two distinguished teachers, of ancient or modern times, agree in their expression of this truth.

For Parker, the authority of Jesus rested in the truths he taught and shared, not in his person. Analogy was made to scientific truth.

Yet, it seems difficult to conceive any reason why moral and religious truths should rest for their support on the personal authority of their revealer, any more than the truths of science on that of him who makes them known first or most clearly. . . . The authority of Jesus, as of all teachers, one would naturally think, must rest on the truth of his words, and not their truth on his authority.

Christianity, Parker proclaimed, was not founded upon the authority of the scriptures or Christ.

So if it could be proved—as it cannot,—in opposition to the greatest amount of historical evidence ever collected on any similar point, that the gospels were the fabrication of designing and artful men, that Jesus of Nazareth had never lived, still Christianity would stand firm, and fear no evil. None of the doctrines of that religion would fall to the ground; for if true, they stand by themselves. If Christianity were true, we should still think it was so, not because its record was written by infallible pens; nor because it was lived out by an infallible teacher,—but that it is true, like the axioms of geometry, because it is true, and is to be tried by the oracle God placed in the breast [intuition].

"The time will come," assured Parker, "when men shall see Christ also as he is." In the meantime, "we have made him an idol." He was great, good, and noble, and "so much of the Divinity was in him"; but we must be careful of making him something he was not.

Measure him by the world's greatest sons,—how poor they are! Try him by the best of men,—how little and low they appear! Exalt him as much as we may, we shall yet, perhaps, come short of the mark. But still was he not our brother; the son of man, as we are; the Son of God, like ourselves? His excellence,—was it not human excellence? His wisdom, love, piety,—sweet and celestial as they were,—are they not what we also may attain?

Believing in and living by true religion—that which is permanent—allows for freedom and variety.

It allows perfect freedom. It does not demand all men to think alike, but to think uprightly, and yet as near as possible at truth; not all men to live alike, but to live holy, and get as near as possible to a life perfectly divine. . . . But Christianity gives us the largest liberty of the sons of God; and were all men Christians after the fashion of Jesus, this variety would be a thousand times greater than now; for Christianity is not a system of doctrines, but rather a method of attaining oneness with God. It demands, therefore, a good life of piety within, of purity without, and gives the promise that who does God's will, shall know of God's doctrine.

Parker spoke of salvation, declaring "it is not so much by the Christ who lived so blameless and beautiful eighteen centuries ago, that we are saved directly, but by the Christ we form in our hearts and live out in our daily life, that we save ourselves, God working with us, both to will and to do." Choosing, believing in, and following the permanent, rather than the transient, provides security.

If you receive the notions about Christianity which chance to be current in your sect or church, solely because they are current, and thus accept the commandment of men instead of God's truth . . . you will be afraid of every new opinion, lest it shake down your church; you will fear "lest if a fox go up, he will break down your stone wall." . . . If on the other hand, you take the true word of God, and live out this, nothing shall harm you.

Parker closed his sermon with a warning to the young man being ordained, and to the several other ministers in attendance. He was concerned about those clergy who knew and believed the things of which he spoke, but were afraid to speak them from their pulpits.

And alas for that man who consents to think one thing in his closet and preach another in his pulpit! God shall judge him in his mercy; not man in his wrath. But over his study and over his pulpit might be writ—EMPTINESS; and on his canonical robes, on his forehead and right hand—DECEIT, DECEIT.

Turning to the congregation, Parker challenged: "You may encourage your brother to tell you the truth. . . . You will then have his best words, his brightest thoughts, and his most hearty prayers."

Daniel Ross Chandler has judged this sermon to be "among the most significant sermons in American intellectual history."[25] William R. Hutchinson has noted that Parker's "Transient and Permanent" sermon marked the beginning of "the great trauma of mid-nineteenth century Unitarianism."[26] The sensation it created was enormous. The first to react were the orthodox Christians who were not Unitarians. In essence, they responded, "we told you so!" Christian liberalism—a designation placed upon and readily accepted by all Unitarians—could only lead, the orthodox asserted, to the eventual rejection of all basic tenets of the Christian faith. The next wave of criticism came from other Unitarians who found themselves in a very difficult position. They prized liberalism and free inquiry, but Parker, they feared, had gone too far. He was too liberal and had strayed far beyond the wide boundaries most Unitarians had established. The great majority of Unitarian pulpits in the Boston area were closed to the young preacher from West Roxbury. One Unitarian layman exclaimed, "I would rather see every Unitarian congregation in our land dissolved and every one of our churches razed to the ground, than to assist in placing a man entertaining the sentiments of Theodore Parker in one of our pulpits."[27] In the *Examiner*, a highly respected Unitarian publication, A. P. Peabody wrote that what Parker had said was all well and good, "but call it Christianity? It was all known before Christ; and, as Mr. Parker justly deems, is known independently of Christ. . . . To give it one name rather than another, is a mere matter of fancy."[28] Even some whom Parker considered as friends, who shared many of the West Roxbury minister's convictions, began to distance themselves from Parker. One such friend, the Reverend Sam Jo May, called

Parker's ordination discourse "a beautiful sermon," but feared that Parker may have sealed his own doom. Parker complained: "As far as ministers are concerned, I am alone, ALL ALONE." That was not entirely true. There were those who stood by him, though most did not.[29] Parker was stung by the criticism, even moved to tears, a reaction not uncommon for the man. Parker was a sensitive person and the barbs of others deeply hurt him. Nevertheless, he refused to be deterred from speaking his convictions and doing what he felt to be right. His congregation at West Roxbury, for the most part, supported him. The few church members he lost were more than replaced by newcomers who were enamored by this unique man with a novel theology.

A Discourse Of Matters Pertaining To Religion (1842)

Parker was invited to deliver a series of five lectures on theology during the winter of 1841–1842 at the Old Masonic Hall in Boston. It was an opportunity for Parker to answer his critics and to expand on the controversial ideas he had presented the previous spring. The hall, with a seating capacity of 750, was nearly filled for every lecture, lending assurance to Parker that there was an audience that wanted to hear his thoughts. John Weiss, a contemporary and early biographer of Parker, noted: "The young men walked in from Cambridge, and back again over the long bridge in the darkness, with hearts aflame. All the earnest thinkers came to hear what he had to say, and many a girl who is now a noble mother, and many strong women whose names have since stood for some humanity of letters or life."[30]

The winter lectures were published in the spring of 1842 in a book entitled, *A Discourse of Matters Pertaining to Religion*. The publication proved to be an expansion upon and elaboration of "The Transient and Permanent in Christianity." Parker attacked contemporary ecclesiology and theology ranging from Calvinism to Unitarianism. Much that he knew, heard, and read about religion seemed at best only tradition, at worst hypocrisy. He reaffirmed the validity of intuition (conscience or reason) above all other forms of revelation. The true word of God, he asserted, came through man's conscience or reason rather than a book.

Man is greater than the Bible. . . . The Bible is made for man, not man for the Bible. . . . Let its errors and absurdities no longer be forced on the pious mind . . . let the word of God come through conscience, reason, and holy feeling, as light through the windows of morning. The knowledge of God's existence, therefore, may be called in the language of philosophy, an intuition of reason.[31]

It was not that Parker believed experience and inductive reasoning could be ignored. Some Transcendentalists could justly be accused of adopting such a position, but not Parker. In his sermons, addresses and writings he used the inductive process to bolster intuitionalist arguments so that they might appear reasonable and scientifically respectable. Parker argued that "the transcendental philosophy . . . does not neglect experience. In human history it finds confirmations, illustrations, of the ideas of human nature. . . . It illustrates religion by facts of observation, facts of testimony." Parker looked to and used the facts of history and science to confirm "the primitive gospel God wrote on the heart of his child." Sometime in the future, Parker attested, a true system of theology and ethics might be attained "by observation and reasoning;" but for the foreseeable future, "the great truths of morality and religion . . . are perceived intuitively, and by instinct."[32]

The churches, according to Parker, had become corrupted and will, therefore, die; true religion, based on reason and intuition will endure.

Blessed was the Christian church while all were brothers. But soon as the Trojan horse of an organized priesthood was dragged through the ruptured wall, there came out of it, stealthily, men cunning as Ulysses, cruel as Diomed, arrogant as Samuel, exclusive and jealous, armed to the teeth in the panoply of worldliness. . . .

Religion, as reason, is of God; the absolute religion, and therefore eternal, based on God alone; the Christian churches, Catholic and Protestant, are of men, and therefore transient.

. . . religion is above all institutions, and can never fail; they shall perish, but religion endures . . . they shall be changed, and the places that knew them shall know them no more forever; but religion is ever the same, and its years shall have no end.[33]

Parker condemned all the various divisions of the Church as having corrupted the true religion of Christ. Of the Catholic Church, he asserted:

The church was the exclusive vicar of God. . . . To accomplish this end, she burnt men. . . . put prophets in chains. . . . emancipated the clergy from the secular law, then giving them license to sin. It sold heaven to extortioners for a little gold, and built St. Peters with the spoil. . . . The church boasts of its uniform doctrine, but it changes every age. . . . The church came at length to be a colossus of crime, with a thin veil of hypocrisy drawn over its face. . . . The catholic church is based on the assumption that God inspires that church, miraculously and exclusively. This assumption is false. Though the oldest organization in the world, it has no right over the soul of man.[34]

When Parker spoke of Calvinism, that system of theology that dominated New England for scores of years, he spared no words. Perhaps reflecting upon the frightening Calvinist preachers he heard in his youth, Parker leveled his verbal guns.

This system degrades Man. . . . It can justify anything out of the Bible. It wars to the knife against gaiety of heart; condemns amusements as sinful; sneers at Common Sense; spits upon Reason, appeals to low and selfish aims—to Fear, the most selfish and base of all passions. . . . It makes religion unnatural to men, and of course hostile. It paves Hell with children's bones; has a personal Devil in the world, to harry the land, and lure or compel men to eternal woe. Its God is diabolical. . . . It makes men stiff, unbending, cold, formal, austere, seldom lovely. They have the strength of the Law, not the beauty of the Gospel; the cunning of the Pharisee, not the simplicity of the Christ. You know its followers as soon as you see them; the rose is faded out of their cheeks; their mouths drooping and sad; their appearance says, Alas, my fellow-worm, there is no more sunshine, for the world is damned. . . . Its Christianity is frozen mercury in the bosom of the warm-hearted Christian, who by nature would go straight to God. The heaven of this system is a grand pay-day . . . the Saints and Martyrs, who bore the trials of the world, are to take their vengeance by shouting "Hallelujah, Glory to God" when they see the anguish of their old persecutors, and the smoke of their torment ascending up for ever and ever.[35]

Even the Unitarians were not spared the preacher's judgment. They, it seemed, had trapped themselves in a web of inconsistencies.

With a philosophy too rational to go the full length of the supernatural theory, too sensual to embrace the spiritual method, and ask no person to mediate between man and God, it oscillates between the two; humanizes the Bible, yet calls it miraculous; believes in man's greatness, freedom, and spiritual nature, yet asks for a Mediator and Redeemer. It censures the traditionary sects, yet sits among the tombs and mourns over things past and gone; believes in the humanity of Jesus, yet his miraculous birth likewise and miraculous powers, and makes him an anomalous and impossible being. It binds men's eyes with the letter, yet bids them look out for the spirit; stops their ears with the texts of the Old Testament, and then asks them to listen to the voice of God in their heart; it reverences Jesus manfully, yet denounces all such as preach Absolute Religion and Morality, as he did, on its own authority. Well might Jeremiah say of it, "Alas for thee, now thou has forsaken the promise of thy youth."[36]

As for members of the human species, there could be no limits on their quest for progress and fulfillment. "The religious teachings of Jesus have this chief excellence," proclaimed Parker, "they allow men to advance indefinitely beyond him."[37] He then went on to relate what the religion of Jesus really was. "Whatever is consistent with reason, conscience, and the religious faculty, is consistent with the Christianity of Jesus, all else is hostile; whoever obeys these three oracles is essentially a Christian, though he lived ten thousand years before Jesus, or living now, does not own his name."[38]

The verbal and written attacks upon Parker from his peers among the Unitarian clergy after publication of *A Discourse* were relentless. One wrote a letter to Parker, declaring: "Sir, I take the liberty to state that your clerical robes are too transparent to conceal the viperous serpents that nestle in your bosom and twine around your heart." Another cleric, in a sermon, declared: "Hell never vomited forth a more blasphemous monster than Theodore Parker." Yet another prayed: "O Lord, if this man is beyond the reaching of the saving influence of the Gospel, remove him out of the way and let his influence die with him."[39] Though such ecclesiastical judgments deeply hurt him, unlike his friends Emerson and George Ripley who abandoned the Church, Parker chose to stay within the Church and work for reform.

In January 1843 accusations of heresy culminated in what could be described as an informal heresy trial of Parker. Members of the Boston Association of Ministers (Unitarian) invited the young minister to tea and discussion at the home of the Reverend Waterston. The meeting was called as a defensive measure on the part of these Unitarian ministers who were troubled that Parker's well-publicized views were casting negative aspersions on the entire Unitarian movement. The pastor from West Roxbury, it was believed, had "introduced discord into the Unitarian body." The Reverend Nathaniel L. Frothingham, who represented the more conservative wing among Boston Unitarians, stated the case: "He that rejects the church, must not belong to it. If he wishes to throw stones at the windows, he must go outside." Commager has summarized the charges and purpose of the meeting: "Mr. Parker was not a Christian, for he denied miracles; Mr. Parker was not a Unitarian, for he denied Christ; the differences between Mr. Parker and the Association was the difference between no Christianity and Christianity. . . . since Mr. Parker compromised the Association, he would do well to withdraw."[40]

Theodore Parker more than held his own at the "trial." If members of the Boston Association did not want to exchange pulpits with him, he understood. They had a right to their decisions. On the other hand, Parker pointed out, he did not know that the Association maintained a right of censorship over its members. He would not withdraw from the Association, but if the Association wished to expel him, then that would be their resolution of the matter. The debate continued for three hours. When it concluded, no decision was made, and cordial handshakes were extended between Parker and his accusers. "Frothingham . . . took Parker by the hand and assured him of his esteem. And so the great heresy trial came to an end on a note of bathos."[41] Parker was never formally expelled from the Unitarian ministry, but from the publication of *A Discourse* he was in actuality an independent preacher.

Exhausted by the controversy and overwork, Parker, in the summer of 1843, boarded a ship in order to spend a year in Europe. When he returned in September of 1844, Parker soon discovered that many had neither forgotten nor forgiven his theological deviancy. In November, the Reverend John Sargent was forced to resign from his church because he had participated in a pulpit exchange with Parker. Towards the end of December, it was Parker's turn to preach the traditional "Great and Thursday Lecture" in the First Church of Boston. His sermon, "The Relation of Jesus to His Age and the Ages," rekindled previous heresy charges. In the sermon Parker acknowledged Jesus as the highest achievement of the human race, though he was persecuted and put to death by the religious sectarians of his day. Jesus, however, was not to be worshipped as God. "That God has yet greater men in store," Parker emphasized, "I doubt not; to say this is not to detract from the majestic character of Christ, but to affirm the omnipotence of God. When they come, the old contest will be renewed—the living prophet stoned, the dead one worshipped."[42] Shortly after this sermon, the Boston Association voted to exclude Parker from further participation in the lectures. In January 1845, Parker exchanged pulpits with James Freeman Clarke, after which fifteen prominent families left Clarke's church.

Parker's efforts toward theological reform in the Unitarian Church would, in the long run, prove successful, reinforcing Parker's own declarations that theology—despite denials in many quarters—was in a constant state of flux. Commager has evaluated: "His [Parker's] theological dissertations and his sermons mark the final emancipation of New England Unitarians from orthodoxy."[43] In 1845, Parker and several devoted followers organized a new congregation, the Twenty-eighth Congregational Society. A group of clergy and laymen had determined "that the Reverend Theodore Parker shall have a chance to be heard in Boston."[44] The congregation first met at the Melodeon Theater in Boston, a huge building, used for vaudeville-type acts during the week. It was poorly ventilated, hot in the summer and cold in the winter. Nevertheless, the Melodeon was soon filled to capacity every Sunday. The people of Boston, representing every strata of life, wanted to hear this man who many had accused of gross heresy. On the first Sunday of 1846, Parker was officially installed as the minister of the Twenty-eighth Congregational Society. Parker himself delivered the installation sermon, "The True Idea of the Christian Church." The sermon provided an opportunity for Parker, then thirty-five years of age, to share his vision of what a church should be, and it became a prophecy of what was to come in Parker's ministry.

A Christian church should be a means of reforming the world, of forming it after the patterns of Christian ideas. It should therefore bring up the sentiments of the times, to judge them by the universal standard. In this way it will learn much and be a living church, that grows with the advance of men's sentiments, ideas and actions, and while it keeps the good of the past will lose no brave spirit of the present day. It can teach much; now moderating the fury of men, then quickening their sluggish steps. We expect the sins of commerce to be winked at in the street; the sins of the State to be applauded on election days and in Congress, or on the Fourth of July; we are used to hear them called the righteousness of the nation. There they are often measured by the avarice or the ambition of greedy men. You expect them to be tried by passion, which looks only to immediate results and partial ends. Here they are to be measured by conscience and reason, which look to permanent results and universal ends; to be looked at with reference to the laws of God, the everlasting ideas on which alone is based the welfare of the world. . . . If the church be true, many things which seem gainful in the street and expedient in the senate-house, will here be set down as wrong, all gain which comes therefrom seem to be but a loss. If there be a public sin in the land, if a lie invade the State, it is for the Church to give the alarm; it is here that it may war on lies and sins, the more widely they are believed in and practiced, the more are they deadly, the more to be opposed. Here let no false idea or fake action of the public go without exposure and rebuke. But let no noble heroism of the times, no noble man pass by with due honor. . . . The noblest monument to Christ, the fairest trophy of religion, is a noble people, where all are well fed and clad, industrious, free, educated, manly, pious, wise, and good.[45]

In 1852 the congregation moved to the new Music Hall where 3,000 people attended almost every Sunday to hear Theodore Parker's brilliant sermons. The congregation "included William Lloyd Garrison, Samuel Gridley Howe, Francis Jackson, Frank B. Sanborn, John C. Holmes, Charles Ellis, Julia Ward Howe, and Caroline Taylor."[46] The crowds continued until 1859 when failing health forced the minister to take leave from his church.

SOCIAL REFORM

As he had boldly stated in his installation sermon, it was not just ecclesiastical or theological reform that was important to Parker. He was consumed by a desire that all society become more just and humane, the kingdom of God on earth. He often spoke in wonderment and sadness that others were not equally passionate about social reform. It was not just clergymen who had this moral responsibility, but all people of learning. Parker had little patience with those who, in their desire to be objective, failed to proclaim an ethical stance. On one occasion he spoke of the responsibility of historians in this regard.

In telling what has been, the historian is also to tell what ought to be, for he is to pass judgments on events, and try counsels by their causes first and their consequence not less. When all these things are told, history ceases to be a mere panorama of events; it become philosophy teaching by experience, and has a profound meaning and awakens a deep interest, while it tells the lessons of the past for the warning of the present and the edification of the future.[47]

Parker believed that clergymen had a special calling to address social issues. Near the end of his life he wrote: "It is idle to say the minister must not meddle in practical things. If the sun is to shine in heaven, it must look into the street, and the shop, and the cellar."[48] On November 18, 1860, Wendell Phillips was in the pulpit at the Music Hall, where he recalled the late Parker's involvement in social reform. "Theodore Parker," Phillips announced, "did not fill these walls because of his unmatched pulpit talents," but because he preached upon "the whole encyclopedia of morals—social questions, sanitary matters, slavery, temperance, labor, the condition of women, the nature of the Government, responsibility to law, the right of a majority, and how far a minority may yield, marriage, health,—the entire list." Phillips could only wish that all preachers understood and practiced social responsibility as Parker did. "If this were recognized and acted upon," Phillips proclaimed, "people would not desert the Church, as they tend to do; or go, if at all, from a mere sense of duty; but would be drawn to the pulpit as they are to the press and theater, by a felt want."[49]

Parker lived at a juncture in American history that was permeated by great reformers: Wendell Phillips, Charles Sumner, William Lloyd Garrison, George Ripley, Ralph Waldo Emerson, Horace Mann, James Russell Lowell, William Ellery Channing, Margaret Fuller, Orestes Brownson, Harriet Beecher Stowe,

Dorthea Dix, and so many others; each in his and her own way a radical. Parker knew most of them, sympathized and worked with many. There was hardly an area left untouched by Parker's scrutiny and critical judgments: poverty, drunkenness, ignorance, prostitution, political corruption, and the plight of women. He joined with those who would abolish capital punishment. He criticized men who paid low wages and high dividends; those who collected exorbitant rentals for wretched slums; bankers who charged high interest rates; lawyers who would defend, for the right price, the worst causes; judges who thought it a crime to be poor; statesmen who made war and called it honorable. He passed strong judgment upon a criminal justice system that neither prevented crime nor reformed criminals; punishment based upon hate and revenge, not upon love and respect for the dignity of man. For Parker, at the heart of almost every social evil was the inordinate desire for wealth. This was a theme to which he returned again and again.

. . . there are exceptional desires; one of which, with the American nation at present, is the desire for wealth. . . . This is the desire of a majority of the young men of talent, ambition and education. Even in colleges more respect is paid to money than to genius. The purse is put before the pen. In the churches, wealth is deemed better than goodness or piety. . . . Money controls the law as well as the gospel.[50]

"A Sermon Of Merchants" (1846)

On Sunday, November 30, 1846, at the Melodeon, Parker delivered a sermon titled, "A Sermon of Merchants," a widely distributed sermon that created quite a sensation in Boston and much of New England. Building on his frequently stated theme that the inordinate desire for and accumulation of wealth was the source of most evils in America, Parker laid much of the blame on the nation's merchants, who were disproportionately located in New England.

The merchant class, according to Parker, was "the most powerful and commanding in society." In the United States, it attracted the most talented and ambitious people. "Commerce and manufacturers offer the most brilliant awards—wealth. . . . Accordingly the ablest men go into the class of merchants. The strongest men in Boston, taken as a body, are not lawyers, doctors, clergymen, book-wrights, but merchants."[51]

The merchant class controlled the nation's political machinery. "It can manufacture governors, senators, judges, to suits its purposes, as easily as it can make cotton cloth. It pays them money and honors, pays them for doing its work." Parker continued: "Our popular legislators are made in its image, represent its wisdom, foresight, patriotism, and conscience."[52]

The merchant class controlled the nation's churches and clergymen, accused Parker. "It buys up the clergymen, hunting them out all over the land; the clergymen who will do its work, putting them in comfortable places. It drives off such as interfere with its work." All this, according to Parker, because "the merchants build mainly the churches, endow theological schools; they furnish the material sinews of the church."[53]

Worst of all, noted Parker, the employees and workers are "at the employer's mercy. . . . There is a strong temptation to use one's power of nature or position to the disadvantage of the weak." Such a temptation was too often yielded to in both South and North.

> In the Southern States, the merchant . . . owns men and deals in their labor, or their bodies. . . . That is slavery. He steals the man and his labor. Here it is possible to do a similar thing. . . . It is possible to employ men and give them just enough of the result of their labor to keep up a miserable life, and yourself take all the rest of the results of that labor. . . . This is not slavery, though only one remove from it. This is the tyranny of the strong over the weak; the feudalism of money; stealing a man's work, and not his person.[54]

Parker noted that at the beginning of the nation's history, it was the colonial merchants who were the reformers. They led the revolt against the tyranny of British nobles. But when this class ascended to power, they become the new oppressors. Once they were leaders in declaring that "all men are born equal, each with unalienable rights; that is self-evident." Now, Parker emphasized, they proclaim, "All dollars are equal, however got; each has unalienable rights. Let no man question that!"[55]

Parker declared that he was not attempting to set "the poor against the rich," but rather "I am trying to set the strong in favor of the weak. . . . to see that no class appropriates to itself what God meant for all." The preacher challenged the merchant class "to organize the rights of man. . . . If this be not done," Parker warned, "the fault is yours. If the nation plays the tyrant over her weakest child, if she plunder and rob the feeble Indian, the feebler Mexican, the Negro, feebler yet, why the blame is yours." Assuming the robes of an Old Testament prophet, Parker thundered: "Remember there is a God who deals; justly with strong and weak. The poor and the weak have loitered behind in the march of men. . . . It is for you, ye elder brothers, to lead forth the weak and poor!" Drawing his sermon to a close—partly warning, partly pleading—Parker said to the merchant class:

> To this class let me say: Remember your Position at the head of the nation; use it, not as pirates, but Americans, Christians, men. . . . And you, my brothers, what shall you become? Not knaves, higgling rather than earn; not tyrants, to be feared whilst living, and buried at last amid popular hate, but men, who thrive best by justice, conscience, and have now the blessedness of just men making themselves perfect.[56]

"The Public Education of the People" (1849)

On October 4, 1849, Parker delivered an oration before the Onondaga Teachers Institute at Syracuse, New York. Entitled, "The Public Education of the

People," Parker's theme was that the education of all the people was a fundamental function of the State, defining education as "the developing and furnishing of the faculties of man."[57] Noting that in other civilizations and cultures, the state only educated a certain class of people—the clergy, the military, the aristocrats—"a Democracy demands the EDUCATION OF ALL." Such a practice works for "the advantage of the State" and "the advantage of the individual himself, irrespective of the State." Parker continued: "The Democratic State has never done its political and educational duty until it affords every man a chance to obtain the greatest amount of education which the attainment of mankind renders it possible for the nation, in its actual circumstances, to command, and the man's nature and disposition render it possible for him to take."[58] The State must, according to Parker, provide "free common schools, free high schools, and free colleges."[59] If the State fails to provide a free education for all at every level, "the rich will have a monopoly of superior education."[60]

Other institutions in society cannot be trusted to provide a proper education. Certainly, the Church cannot.

The Churches have little love of Truth. . . . They promote only popular forms of truth, popular in all Christendom, or in their special sect. . . . They dishonor free thinking, and venerate constrained believing. When the clergy doubt, they seldom give men audience of their doubt. . . . No great moral movement of the age is at all dependent directly on the Church for its development. It is in spite of the Church that reforms go forward.[61]

Neither can Business be trusted to provide adequate education, for "it does not tend to promote the highest forms of character."

It does not lead the employer to help the operative as a man, only to use him as a tool. . . . The average merchant cares little whether his ship brings cloth and cotton, or opium and rum. . . . The ordinary manufacturer is as ready to make cannons and cannon-balls to serve in a war which he knows is unjust, as to cast his iron into mill-wheels, or forge it into anchors. The common farmer does not care whether his barley feeds poultry for the table, or, made into beer, breeds drunkards for the almshouses and the jail; asks not whether his rye and potatoes become the bread of life, or, distilled into whiskey, are deadly poison to men and women.[62]

The Press, for all the good it accomplishes, does "little to elevate men above the present standards."

The political journals have the general vice of our Politics, and the special faults of the particular party; the theological journals have the common failings of the Church, intensified by the bigotry of the sects they belong to; the commercial journals represent the bad qualities of Business.[63]

Parker emphasized that "the teachers in the schools should be of such a character that they can give the children what they will most want when they become men."[64] To be certain that he was not misunderstood, Parker wanted it known that when "I say every man, I mean every woman also,"[65] thus demonstrating his often expressed concern about the demeaning place of women in society. Again, he stressed the importance of the quality of teachers.

We need able men, well endowed by nature, well disciplined by art; we need superior men—men juster than the State, truer and better than the Churches, more humane than Business, and higher than the common literature of the Press. . . . How shall we bring them to the task? Give young men and women the opportunity to fit themselves for the work, at free Common Schools, High Schools, Normal Schools, and Colleges, give them a pay corresponding to their services . . . give them social rank and honor . . . and they will come.[66]

Parker took time in his speech to recognize the heroic efforts of Horace Mann in promoting adequate education.

It seems strange that so few great men in Politics have cared much for the education of the People; only one of those now prominent before the North, is intimately connected with it. He, at great personal sacrifice of money, of comfort, of health, even of respectability, became Superintendent of the Common Schools of Massachusetts, a place, whence we could ill spare him, to take the place of the noble man he succeeds. Few of the prominent scholars of the land, interest themselves in the public education of the People. The men of superior culture think the Common School beneath their notice; but it is the mother of them all.[67]

Parker concluded his address by challenging the educators before him.

Men and women, practical teachers now before me, a great trust is in your hands; nine–tenths of the children of the People, depend on you for their early culture, for all the scholastic discipline they will ever get; their manly culture will depend on that, their prosperity thereon, all these on you. When they are men, you know what evils they will easily learn from State and Church, from Business and the Press. It is for you to give them such a developing and such a furnishing of their powers, that they will withstand, counteract and exterminate that evil.[68]

For all the social issues that Parker addressed, it was the North–South crisis to which he devoted most of his oratorical attention: slavery, sectionalism, and the ever increasing possibility of a civil war.

Slavery

It was for slavery that Parker reserved his severest judgments and harshest words. For him, slavery was "the sum of all villainies," and his greatest and most courageous efforts were directed towards its abolishment. He delivered his first antislavery sermon January 31, 1841. In that sermon, Parker laid the blame for slavery on economics, the same source, according to the preacher, of all other social evils. "The plain truth of the matter is this:—men who wish for wealth and luxury, but hate the toil and sweat, which are their natural price, brought the African to America; they made his chains, they live by his tears; they dance to the piping of his groans; they fatten on his sweat and are pampered by his blood."[69]

In that first slavery sermon Parker spoke to those in the North who refused to address themselves to the matter of slavery. His arguments follow the patterns of classical refutation. To those who pleaded that many slave masters were "excellent Christians," Parker replied: " . . . a sin is a sin though a Christian commit it. Our fathers did not think that 'taxation without representation' any the less an evil because imposed by 'his most Christian Majesty,' a king of Christians." To those who argued that the slaves were happy, well-fed, and clothed, Parker responded that you can't weigh "a good . . . against freedom!" To those who claimed that the sufferings of slaves were exaggerated, Parker answered: " . . . though there have been exaggerations in details, yet the awful sum of misery, unspeakable wretchedness, which hangs over two million slaves is such that eye hath not seen it." To those who claimed that the North should have nothing to say about slavery because it was an affair of the South, of slaveholders, and their slaves, Parker rejoined that because the North profited by the institution of slavery it was the North's affair. Then he proclaimed: "If there is a crime in the land known to us, and we do not protest against it to the extent of our ability, we are partners of that crime."[70]

The Mexican War caused Parker to renew his attacks upon slavery. He denounced it as a war to extend the boundaries of slavery. On February 4, 1849, he delivered an address at Faneuil Hall where he thundered, "This war is waged for a mean and infamous purpose, for the extension of slavery. . . . we must have yet more land to whip negroes in."[71] It was a courageous stance to speak against a war that had much popular support throughout the nation. Soldiers with bayonets surrounded the meeting at Fanueil Hall. Parker took notice in his address. "Here are soldiers with bayonets to overawe the majesty of the people."[72] Parker was aware that President Polk had said that opposition to the war was treason. "Your President tells it is treason to talk so! Treason is it? . . . If my country is wrong, and I know it, and hold my peace, then I am guilty of treason, moral treason."[73]

The history of the United States, according to Parker, was a history of freedom versus slavery, with slavery being the winner most of the time. In an address in December of 1848, Parker said that slavery won its first battle in the United States Constitution.

In 1787, the best and most celebrated statesmen were publicly active on the side of freedom. Some thought slavery a sin, others a mistake, but nearly all in the Convention thought it an error. South Carolina and Georgia were the only States thoroughly devoted to slavery at that time. They threatened to withdraw from the Union if it were not sufficiently respected in the new Constitution. If the other States had said, "You may go, soon as you like, for hitherto you have been only a curse to us, and done little but brag," it would have been better for us all. However, partly for the sake of keeping the peace, and still more for the purpose of making money by certain concessions to the South, the North granted the Southern demands.[74]

In an address delivered to the New England Anti-Slavery Convention on May 29, 1850, Parker listed the other losses for the cause of freedom to slavery in addition to the Constitution: the acquisition of Louisiana and Florida as slave territories; the Missouri Compromise; the annexation of Texas as a slave state; and the Mexican War whose purpose was the extension of slavery. Since the Revolution, Parker could think of only three instances where freedom had beaten back slavery: the prohibiting of slavery from the Northwest Territory, before the adoption of the Constitution; the prohibiting of the slave-trade in 1808; and the prohibition of slavery in Oregon.[75]

In that same sermon Parker announced that slavery was supported by both of the contemporary political parties.

Neither of the great political parties is hostile to slavery. That institution has the continual support of both the Whig and Democratic parties. . . . In the Senate of the United States, only Seward and Chase and Hale can be counted on as hostile to slavery. In the House, there are Root and Giddings and Wilmont and Mann, and a few others. "But what are these among so many?"[76]

Parker spoke of William Lloyd Garrison with words of high praise. "There rose up one man who would not compromise, nor be silent,—who would be heard. . . . He found a few others, a very few, and began the anti-slavery movement."[77] Parker was equally complimentary toward all those who assumed places of leadership in the abolitionist movement. "One thing must be said of the leaders of the anti-slavery movement," Parker exclaimed, "they ask for nothing but justice; not justice for themselves . . . but only justice for the slave; and to obtain that, they forsook all that human hearts must love."[78]

In his praise for the abolitionists, Parker separated himself from most other prominent antislavery preachers, such as Henry Ward Beecher and Charles Finney, who looked upon Garrison and other abolitionists as being too radical. Parker's admiration for the abolitionists was affirmed as early as his first sermon against slavery in 1841.

We all know there is at the North a small body of men, called by various names, and treated with various marks of disrespect, who are zealously striving to procure the liberation of slaves, in a peaceful and quiet way. They are willing to make sacrifices for this end. They start from the maxim that slavery is a sin, and that sin is to be abandoned at once, and for ever. . . . What wonder is it that these men sometimes grow warm in their arguments! What wonder that their heart burns when they think of so many women exposed to contamination and nameless abuse; of so many children reared like beasts, and sold as oxen; of so many men owning no property in their hands, or their feet, their hearts, or their lives.[79]

Parker leveled scathing attacks against the Fugitive Slave Law of 1850 which he considered a gross evil not to be tolerated. The thought of northern citizens sending escaped slaves, fugitives, back to the South in chains was a wrong almost beyond Parker's comprehension. In a sermon at the Melodeon on Sunday, September 22, 1850, Parker expressed his personal determination to disobey the hated law.

I will do all in my power to rescue any fugitive slave from the hands of any officer who attempts to return him to bondage. I will resist him as gently as I know how, but work with such strength as I can command; I will ring bells and alarm the town; I will serve as head, as foot, or as hand to any body of serious men, who will go with me, with no weapons in their hands, in this work. I will do it as readily as I would lift a man out of the water, or pluck him from the teeth of a wolf, or snatch him from the hands of a murderer.[80]

In another sermon at the Melodeon, on April 10, 1851, Parker urged others to resist the law. "What shall we do?" he asked. "Never obey the law. Keep the law of God." Yet, he urged that resistance stop short of violence. "Do not resist with violence," he implored. "It is not time just yet; it would not succeed. Resist then, by peaceful means."[81] It is important to note that Parker's reservation about violence was not moral but utilitarian.

In reaction to the Fugitive Slave Law, Parker helped to organize the Boston Vigilance Committee which aided former slaves to escape capture. He hid many blacks in his home until they could find a more secure place. All this was carried out in defiance of national law. On November 7, 1850, he secretly presided over the marriage of two fugitives, William and Ellen Craft, before sending them to England. In his journal, Parker cited what happened immediately following the ceremony.

Then I noticed a Bible lying on one table and a sword on the other; I saw them when I first came into the house and determined what use to make of them. I took the Bible, put it into William's right hand, and told him the use of it. . . . I then took the sword; I put that in his hand and told him if the worst came to worst, to use that to save his wife's liberty or her life, if he could effect it no other way. . . . I put into his hands these two dissimilar instruments, one for the body, one for his soul at all events.[82]

In 1855, Parker bore some responsibility (it is still a question as to what degree) for inciting a mob to attempt the rescue of a fugitive, Anthony Burns, from the Boston Courthouse. For this action, Parker, Wendell Phillips, and others were arrested and indicted for obstructing the execution of the Fugitive Slave Law. The charges were dismissed on a legal technicality, but it is generally considered that the prosecutors were most reluctant to press charges against someone with the stature and influence of Parker.

In several sermons and addresses Parker expressed his great agitation about the participation of the North in general, and Boston in particular, with the Fugitive Slave Law.

It was the result of a union of the slave power of the South with the money power of the North.[83]

In the Yankee it has brought out some of the most disgraceful examples of meanness that ever dishonored mankind.[84]

O Boston! Thou wert once the prayer and pride of all New England men. . . . Thou art dishonored now; thou hast taken to thy arms, the enemies of men. Thou hast betrayed the slave. . . . Thou art a stealer of mankind. . . . The golden serpent of commerce has twined its snaky folds about it all, and fascinated into sleep the child.[85]

On April 12, 1852, at the Melodeon, on the first anniversary of the capture and return to slavery of the fugitive, Thomas Simms, Parker lamented over the guilt of Boston. The sermon, entitled "The Boston Kidnapping," besides being a beautiful demonstration of prose, exhibits a fine grasp of history.

Out of the house of bondage, a man, guilty of no crime but love of liberty, fled to the people of Massachusetts. He came to us a wanderer, and Boston took him in to an unlawful jail; hungry, and she fed him with a felon's meat; thirsty, and she gave him the gall and vinegar of a slave to drink; naked, she clothed him with chains; sick and in prison, he cried for a helper, and Boston sent him a marshal and a commissioner; she set him between kidnappers, among the most infamous of men, and they made him their slave. Poor and in chains, the government of the nation against him, he sent round to the churches his petition for their prayers; the churches of commerce, they gave him their curse; he asked of us the sacrament of freedom in the name of our God; and in the name of their trinity, the trinity of money,—Boston standing as godmother at their ceremony,—in the name of their God they baptized him a slave.[86]

Parker condemned Daniel Webster for his part in the passage of the Fugitive Slave Law. On March 7, 1850, Webster had delivered a speech in the United States Senate that disturbed many of his supporters in New England. As a means of trying to compromise with the South in order to save the Union, Webster advocated no restrictions on slavery in New Mexico, upheld the Fugitive Slave Law, and denounced the abolitionist societies in the North for their seditious agitation. Though Webster disliked slavery, he loved the Union more and made his speech to prevent secession which was being threatened at the time by John C. Calhoun and others.

On March 25, at Fanueil Hall, Parker made a stinging reply to Webster. The speech took courage, for Webster, in spite of his compromising address earlier in the month, was still a popular personality in New England. Parker dismantled Webster's argument; even more, he dismantled Webster.

We waited long for his words; we held our peace in his silence; we listened for his counsel. Here it is; adverse to freedom beyond the fear of his friends, and the hopes even of his foes. He has done wrong things before, cowardly things more than once; but this, the wrongest and most cowardly of them all: we did not look for it. . . . his deed is done in the face of the world, and nothing can hide it. . . .

I think this is the only reasonable way in which we can estimate this speech—as a bid for the presidency. . . .

I know of no deed in American history, done by a son of New England, to which I can compare this, but the act of Benedict Arnold.[87]

On October 31, 1852, Parker delivered a discourse occasioned by Webster's death. There was some praise for the deceased in the speech, but even more it expressed great disappointment over the life of Webster, over the contrast between what could have been and what was. Parker spoke of Webster's greatness, but made it clear that it was a greatness of intellect, not of morality.

Of conscience it seemed to me he had little; in his latter life, exceeding little: his moral sense seemed long besotted; almost, though not wholly gone. . . .

What will posterity say of his efforts to chain the fugitive, to extend the area of human bondage; of his haughty scorn of any law higher than what trading politicians enact in the Capitol? . . .

No living man has done so much to debauch the conscience of the nation, to debauch the press, the pulpit, the forum, and the bar. There is no Higher Law, quoth he, and how much of the pulpit, the press, the forum, and the bar denies its God. He poisoned the moral wells of society with his lower law, and men's consciences died of the murrain of beats, which came because they drank thereat.[88]

There were those who denounced Parker for disrespectful speech of the dead. Others, however, had a different reaction. Julia Ward Howe heard the address, then rushed home late for dinner, and exclaimed: "Do not scold me. I have just heard the greatest speech I shall ever hear."[89] Charles Francis Adams wrote to Parker: "Yours is the only independent and thorough analysis that will be made of that gentleman's life."[90]

In his fight against slavery, Parker appealed again and again to a higher law. In his sermon, "The Function of Conscience," he spoke of the higher law which he equated with "the moral law of God." It is important to notice how closely Parker associated the human conscience with the law of God. Once again, the source of authority is intuition.

It is the function of conscience to discover to men the moral law of God. It will not do this with infallible certainty. . . . But conscience, like each other faculty, is relatively perfect,—is adequate to the purpose God meant it to be. . . .

This we need to continually remember: that nothing in the world without is so sacred as the eternal law of God; of the world within nothing is more venerable than our own conscience, the permanent, everlasting oracle of God.[91]

The higher law, according to Parker, should be more binding that one's allegiance to the Constitution or State.

Suppose a man sworn to keep the Constitution of the United States and the Constitution is found to be wrong in certain particulars, then his oath is not morally binding, for before this oath, by his very existence, he is morally bound to keep the law of God as fast as he learns it. No oath can absolve him from his natural allegiance to God.

To say that there is no higher law than what the State can make is practical atheism. It is not a denial of God in his person; this is only speculative atheism. It is a denial of the functions and attributes of God; that is real atheism. If there is no God to make a law for me, then there is no God for me.[92]

The higher law is one of the basic safeguards of society; and if civil law ever conflicts with higher law, it is the higher law that must be obeyed.

... right is divine, is of God, not merely provisional and for to-day, but absolute and for eternity. .... If government, statutes, officers, command me to do right, I must do it, not because commanded, but because it is right; if they command me to do wrong, I must refuse, not because commanded, but because it is wrong.[93]

I love law, and respect law, and should be slow to violate it. .... But when the rulers have inverted their function, and enacted wickedness into a law which treads down the alienable right of man to such a degree as this, then I know no ruler but God, no law but natural justice.[94]

Parker complained that some of the clergy had ignored the higher law. "Some ministers have been silent; others have spoken out in favor of the lower law, and in derision of the higher law."[95] In the whole realm of social reform, and on the slave issue in particular, Parker was convinced that God was marching on but the Church was lagging far behind. He saw the Church as the most conservative of institutions, more concerned with ritual and dogma than with life. He complained that the pulpit in New England was limited and hesitant.

The pulpit is not to be relied on for much aid. If all the minsters of New England were abolitionists, with the same zeal that they are Protestants, Universalists, Methodists, Calvinists, or Unitarians, no doubt the whole state would soon be an anti-slavery State, and the day of emancipation would be wonderfully hastened. But that we are not to look for.[96]

He raised the age-old issue as to whether churches and clergy are molders or reflectors of public opinion. It is an important question and goes to the heart of how much responsibility the churches and clergy must bear for the sectional crisis and if their "sins" were ones of omission or commission. Parker thought, in his day at least, the churches were far more reflectors than shapers.

I am not inclined to attribute so much original power to the churches as some men do. I look on them as indicators of public opinion, and not sources thereof—not the wind, but only the vane which shows which way it blows. Once the clergy were the masters of the people, and the authors of public opinion to a great degree; now they are chiefly the servants of the people, and follow public opinion, and but seldom aspire to lead it, except in matters of their own craft, such as the technicalities of a sect, or the form of a ritual.[97]

In spite of all the indicators to the contrary, Parker was optimistic that the antislavery movement would succeed. Right and the power of God could not fail. In an address delivered at Faneuil Hall, as early as May in 1848, Parker emphasized his convictions.

We are certain of success; the spirit of the age is on our side. See how the old nations shake their tyrants out of the land. . . . do you believe American can keep her slaves? It is idle to think so. So all we want is time. On our side are truth, justice, and the eternal right. Yes, on our side is religion, the religion of Christ; on our side are the hopes of mankind, and the great power of God.[98]

Sectionalism

Theodore Parker did not live long enough to witness the secession of the southern states. He died on May 10, 1860. Seven months after his death, South Carolina, on December 20, 1860, held a state convention and voted to become the first state to secede from the Union. However, Parker had strong views on sectionalism. He saw great differences between the North and South. In an 1850 Thanksgiving sermon, entitled, "The State of the Nation," Parker pointed out differences in origin between the two sections of the nation.

The South, in the main, had a very different origin from the North. . . . few persons settled there for religion's sake; or for the sake of freedom in the State. It was not a moral idea which sent men to Virginia, Georgia, or Carolina. . . . The difference in the seed will appear in the difference of the crop. . . . The South with its despotic idea, dishonors labor, but wishes to compromise between its idleness and its appetite, and so kidnaps men to do its work.[99]

For Parker there was a difference in the history of the two sections. A sermon in December of 1848 entitled "The Free-Soil Movement"—a sermon that smacked of strong provincialism—specified the historical differences.

Who fought the Revolution? Why the North, furnishing the money and the men, Massachusetts alone sending fourteen thousand soldiers more than all the present slave states. Who pays the national taxes? The North, for the slaves pay but a trifle. Who owns the greater part of the property, the mills, the shops, the ships? The North. Who writes the books—the histories, poems, philosophies, works of science, even the sermons and commentaries on the Bible? Still the North. Who sends their children to schools and colleges? The North. Who builds the churches, who founds the Bible societies, missionary societies, the thousand-and-one institutions for making men better and better off? Why the North. In a word, who is it in seventy years has made the nation great, rich, and famous for her ideas and their success all over the world? The answer is still the North, the North.
    Well, says the calculator, but who has the offices of the nation? The South. Who has

filled the presidential chair forty-eight years out of sixty? Nobody but slaveholders. Who has held the chief posts of honor? The South. Who occupy the chief offices in the army and navy? The South. Who increases the cost of the post-office and pays so little of the expense? The South. Who made the Mexican War? The South. Who sets at naught the Constitution? The South. Who would bring the greatest peril in the case of war with a strong enemy? Why the South, the South. But what is the South most noted for abroad? For her three million slaves; and the North for her wealth, freedom, education, religion![100]

In an 1851 sermon, Parker echoed a similar theme. Because the South had disregarded higher law, its society had paid a price: "Ask the Southern States of America to show us their rapid increase in riches, in civilization; to show us their schools and their scholars, their literature, their science, and their art."[101] Nevertheless, Parker lamented that the South was much more committed to its way of life than the North was to its. "Southern slavery is an institution which is in earnest. Northern Freedom is an institution that is not in earnest."[102]

A nation so divided could not stand. On July 11, 1854, Parker delivered a "house-divided" sermon, four years before Lincoln gave an address on a similar theme. "There can be no national welfare without a national unity of action," Parker intoned. "That cannot take place unless there is a national Unity of Idea in fundamentals. Without this a nation is a 'house divided against itself,' of course it cannot stand."[103]

Though he thought the North superior to the South, morally and culturally, Parker did not hesitate to criticize the northern ethic in regard to slavery. He was especially critical of his own area of the nation. In 1848 he declared, "the men who control the politics of Massachusetts, of all New England, do not oppose or dislike slavery."[104] An 1852 address found him particularly disappointed with Boston.

Boston capitalists do not hesitate to own Southern plantations and buy and sell men; Boston merchants do not scruple to let their ships for the domestic slave trade. . . . Most of the slave-ships in the Atlantic are commanded by New England men. . . . The controlling men of Boston have done much to promote, to extend, and to perpetuate slavery. Why not, if interest is before justice? Why not, if the higher law of God is to be sneered at in State and Church?[105]

The controlling classes in both South and North were responsible for the moral ills that plagued the nation. "In America the controlling class is divided into two great parties," declared Parker, "one is the slave power in the States of the South; the other is the money power is the cities of the North. . . . They are hostile to the great idea that is America."[106]

The Coming of War

Parker died before the Civil War began and, therefore, could make no comments on it. He did, however, say much about the use of violence and war, and from these statements one can fairly speculate that Parker would have been an ardent supporter of the war. In reading Parker's comments, whether in private letters or public addresses, it is apparent that a change took place in his thinking concerning war and violence. In his sermon, "War," preached on June 7, 1846, a sermon inspired by troubles with Mexico. Parker was opposed to war and there seemed to be no exceptions. In an impressive massing of statistics, Parker fumed against the destructiveness, the uselessness, and the immorality of war. "War," he said, "is a violation of Christianity. If war be right, then Christianity is wrong, false, a lie. . . . It is a national infidelity, a denial of Christianity and of God."[107] He continued:

We have fewer fleets, forts, canon, and soldiers for the population, than any other Christian country in the world. This is one main reason why we have no national debt. . . . War, wasting a nation's wealth, depresses the great mass of people, but serves to elevate a few to opulence and power. Every despotism is established and sustained by war. . . . Nothing is so hostile to a true democracy as war.[108]

In that same sermon Parker made some brief comments on a "just war." He said that he understood the concept and honored men who upheld such a doctrine, but that he had some reservations about even that kind of war. Three years later, however, Parker was announcing that some wars were worthwhile. On January 4, 1849, he delivered another sermon on the Mexican War. In that sermon, though he continued to perceive that particular war as evil because it extended the boundaries of slavery, he declared that there had been wars that were "worth what they cost. . . . War followed the American Revolution. It cost money, it cost men. But if we calculate; the value of American ideas, they are worth what they cost. Even the French Revolution, with all its carnage, robbery, and butchery, is worth what it cost."[109]

In 1850, Parker preached that war was the only way to settle the struggle between slavery and freedom, the only way to accomplish peace. "We cannot have any unsettled and lasting harmony until one or the other of these ideas is cast out of the councils of the nation: so there must be war between them before there can be peace."[110]

The same transformation of thought is observed in regard to Parker's views on violence. It was noted that in 1851, Parker urged resistance to the Fugitive Slave Law by all means except violence.[111] Even then, however, his caution was not a moral matter. He simply believed that at that time, violence would not work. As the slavery issue continued to inflame the people of the North and South with ever increasing intensity, Parker's reluctance to advocate violence diminished. During one week of the fugitive slave crisis in Boston, Parker wrote his sermons with a loaded pistol on his desk.[112] He became a part of a small committee that supported the various crusades of John Brown. Early in 1857 he wrote to Judge Russell, who at that time was furnishing a hiding place for Brown: "If I were in his [John Brown's] position I should shoot dead anyone who attempted to arrest me for these alleged crimes. . . . P.S. I don't advise J.B. to do this, but it is what I should do."[113] When Brown raided the arsenal at Harper's Ferry, Parker was in Europe, futilely attempting to regain his health. On November 24, 1859, Parker wrote a letter to Francis Jackson. Much of the letter was a justification of Brown's actions, a justification of violence.

It may be a natural duty of the slave to develop this natural right in a practical manner, and actually kill all those who seek to prevent his enjoyment of liberty. . . . It may be a natural duty of the freemen to help slaves to the enjoyment of their liberty, and as a means to that end, to aid them in killing such as oppose their natural freedom.[114]

Parker seemed to be hoping for and advocating a slave insurrection. Furthermore, he believed the white man had a duty to aid the slave in the rebellion. There can be little doubt that Parker, had he lived, would have supported the Civil War; however, whereas the motives of Lincoln and most Union leaders were to save the Union first, with emancipation a secondary motive; for Parker, the priorities would have been reversed.

BIOGRAPHICAL TOPICS

For Parker there was no distinction between the natural and supernatural. All that exists was of God's doing. Therefore, nothing was beyond the interest and attention of the preacher. Such a position separated Parker from most preachers of his day. Phillips Brooks, for example,—who along with Henry Ward Beecher, Sydney E. Ahlstrom labeled as "Princes of the Pulpit" during the nineteenth century[115]—seldom addressed social issues from the pulpit. Though Brooks had strong beliefs about various social and civil matters, and would address them in personal letters and private conversations, he held that "secular" concerns had no place in the "sacred" pulpit. Robert T. Oliver, a scholar of rhetoric, has written: "There was a curious remoteness about the life and preaching of Brooks. . . . he shrank from discussion of current affairs; his business was with eternity."[116] Brooks had a "profound conviction that all improvement in society must be the product of a change in character of the people who compose that society."[117] Of the approximate 550 of Brooks' sermons that remain, only a handful speak to social issues. Many of the sermons do deal with principles and ethical stances that could be applied to so-called secular concerns, but the application was almost never made.[118] Brooks was typical of many clergymen in his era, probably of every era. Not so, Theodore Parker. For him, there was no wall of separation between the sacred and the secular.

Therefore, Parker spoke more often of American personalities than biblical figures. His comments on Daniel Webster, John Brown, and William Lloyd Garrison have already been noted. Few prominent Americans, present or past, escaped his rhetorical attention. For example, after acknowledging and specifying Benjamin Franklin's "little inconsistencies," Parker continued with high praise.

No man ever rendered so great services to American education. . . . His character was singularly simple and healthy. . . . The warning he gives is plain—to beware of excess in early youth, of trifling with the most delicate sensibilities of woman, and of ever neglecting the most sacred duties of domestic life. Few men understood the art of life as well as he. He took great pains to correct his faults. . . . He shows not less the power of justice and benevolence. . . . What a life! What a character![119]

In his memorial of George Washington, Parker sought to refute a few of the criticisms some had made of the man, and then eloquently exalted the first president's character and contributions.

You will say, "he did little for the freedom of the slaves." He did more than all Presidents, with the exception of Jefferson and Madison. Think of any President for forty years daring to call slavery "wicked," "unnatural," to commend emancipation, or liberate his slaves at his death. Some ministers would say, "he hath denied the faith, and is worse than an infidel!" Judge men by their own acts, and by their own light, not by yours or mine. Before he left the earth, he wrenched the fetters from off each bondman's foot, and, as he began his flight to heaven, dropped them down into the bottomless pit of Hell, where they may find who seek. . . .
For one thousand years no king in Christendom has shown such greatness, or gives us so high a type of manly virtue. He never dissembled. He sought nothing for himself. In him there was no unsound spot; nothing little or mean in his character. The whole was clean and presentable. We think better of mankind because he lived, adorning the earth with a life so noble. Shall we make an Idol of him, and worship it with huzzah on the Fourth of July, and with stupid Rhetoric on other days? Shall we build him a great monument, founding it in a slave pen? His glory already covers the Continent. More than two hundred places bear his name. He is revered as "The Father of his Country." The people are his memorial.[120]

In a discourse on Thomas Jefferson, Parker responded to those who labeled the third president an infidel. "We have seen that Mr. Jefferson was a profound and independent thinker," noted Parker; "he called no man master, and among the various sectarians of his day, who would not allow the name of Christian to each other, it cannot be expected that it should have been commonly allowed to him. Yet surely there was a certain piety, and some depth of religious feeling in the man." Parker concluded his remarks on Jefferson with guarded praise.

It may not be said of him that of all those famous men he could least have been spared; for in the rare and great qualities for patiently and wisely conducting the vast affairs of State and Nation in pressing emergencies, he seems to have been wanting. But his grant merit was this—that while his powerful opponents favored a strong government, and believed it necessary thereby to repress what they called the lower classes, he, Jefferson, believed in Humanity; believed in a true Democracy. He respected labor and education, and upheld the right to education of all men. Those were the Ideas in which he was far in advance of all the considerable men, whether of his State or of his Nation—ideas which he illustrated through long years of his life and conduct.[121]

John Quincy Adams died on February 23, 1848, and Parker, on March 5, felt compelled to address the lessons from Adams' life. The two men knew and admired each other. They were fellow Unitarians. An elderly Adams had made the effort to attend the young Parker's ordination and installation service at West Roxbury in 1837.

Parker's memorial discourse on the former president was lengthy, even by Parker's standards. In the address, Parker, as he usually did in speaking of any person, attempted to be objective. This meant noting a person's failings along with his successes and contributions. So, of Adams, Parker noted: "I do not say there were no exceptions to this devotion to freedom in a long life; there are some passages in his history which it is impossible to justify, and hard to excuse. . . . I am not to praise Mr. Adams simply because he is dead; what is wrong before is wrong after death. . . . shall we tell lies about him because he is dead?"[122]

Parker spoke of those "exceptions" in some detail. Senator Adams' support of the 1807 Embargo Act was, according to Parker, Adams' "worst act of his public life; I cannot justify it."[123] Parker was critical of President Adams's failure to recognize the independence of Haiti and his support of England in her war against China. Parker also thought Adams was unjustifiably harsh in dealing with his foes.

He was what is called a good hater. If he loved an idea, he seemed to hate the man who opposed it. . . . In his attacks on persons he was sometimes unjust, violent, sharp, and vindictive; sometimes cruel, and even barbarous. Did he ever forgive an enemy?[124]

Nevertheless, Parker understood, for Adams had "encountered more political opposition than any man in the nation. For more that forty years he has never been without bitter and unrelenting enemies, public and private."[125]

In spite of human failures, Adams was, in Parker's view, a noble man and a great American.

But there is one sentiment which runs through all his life: an intense love of freedom for all men . . . that each man has unalienable rights.[126]

He thought the Indians were unjustly treated, cried out against the wrong.[127]

This sentiment led him to oppose tyranny in the House of Representatives, the tyranny of the majority.[128]

This love of freedom led him to hate and oppose the tyranny of the strong over the weak, to hate it most in its worst form; to hate American Slavery, doubtless the most infamous form of that tyranny . . . and perhaps the most disgraceful thing on earth.[129]

While he was President he would not consent to any "public manifestation of honors personal to himself." He would not accept a present [knowing] that a gift blinds the eyes of wise men and perverts their judgment.[130]

In one thing he surpassed most men,—he grew more liberal the more he grew old, he welcomed new ideas, kept his mind vigorous, and never fell into the crabbed admiration of past times and buried institutions, which is the palsy of so many a man, and which makes old age nothing but a pity, and gray hairs provocative of tears.[131]

Parker noted that Adams "had a high reverence for religion; none of our public men more." By Parker's religious standards, Adams was "rather unphilosophical in his theology, resting to a great degree on the authority of tradition and the letter." Yet, the preacher observed, "you shall find few statesmen, few men, who act with a more continual and obvious reference to religion as a motive, as a guide, as a comfort." Declaring that Adams was "no sectarian," Parker emphasized Adams's strong belief in freedom of religion. "He thought for himself," and "allowed others to think also for themselves, and have a theology of their own." Parker observed that Adams was a Unitarian at a time "when Unitarianism was little, despised, mocked at, and called 'Infidelity.'" Noting that Adams, when Secretary of State, worshipped with a small group of Unitarians in Washington, Parker deducted that Adams "in his theology, as in politics . . . feared not to stand in a minority. If there ever was an American who loved the praise of God more than the praise of men, I believe Mr. Adams was one."[132]

For those having a particular interest in rhetoric, it is important to read what Parker had to say about Adams' eloquence, or more precisely, Adams's lack of it. After stating that Adams was "seldom eloquent," Parker dismissed the gift as of little importance.

Eloquence is no great gift. It has its place among subordinate powers, not among the chief. Alas for the statesman or preacher who had only that to save the State withal! Washington had none of it, yet how he ruled the land! No man in America has ever had a political influence so wide and permanent as Mr. Jefferson; yet he was a very indifferent writer, and never made a speech of any value. The acts of Washington, the ideas of Jefferson, made eloquence superfluous. True, it has its value; if a man have at command the electricity of truth, justice, love, the sentiment and great ideas thereof, it is a good thing to be able with Olympian hand to condense that electric fire into bolted eloquence; to thunder and lighten in the sky. But if a man have that electric truth, it matters little whether it is Moses that speaks, or only Aaron.[133]

Similar assessments on truth as more than compensating for lack of eloquence were made of Parker himself. Drawing his long memorial of Adams to a close, the preacher affirmed:

The slave has lost a champion who gained new ardor and new strength the longer he fought; America has lost a man who loved her with his heart; Religion has lost a supporter; Freedom an unfailing friend, and Mankind a noble vindicator of our unalienable rights. . . . South Carolina need ask no more a halter for that one northern neck she could not bend or break. The tears of his country are dropped upon his urn; the muse of history shall write thereon, in letters not be effaced, THE ONE GREAT MAN SINCE WASHINGTON, WHOM AMERICA HAD NO CAUSE TO FEAR.[134]

There was nothing random or haphazard in Parker's choice of subjects upon which he would preach. He would block out his topics months and often years in advance. He wanted to cover a wide range of truths in some kind of coherent order, and planning well into the future enabled him to do this.[135] The continuity was often interrupted because of pressing issues on the local and national scene that needed to be addressed; but after the interruptions, Parker would return to the broad plan. It was usually in the interruptions where Parker gained his reputation for contentiousness. In the broader plan he was more didactic in nature, the teacher imparting important and necessary truths to his pupils.

It is important to emphasize that most of Parker's orations were not harsh nor denunciatory in nature, for that impression is often conveyed. His controversial and contentious sermons were his most remembered sermons, but they were not the common pattern of his discourses. Parker climbed the mountain of exaltation when he talked about the qualities of God; God's infinite perfection, his mercy, love, and compassion. He was exuberant when he contemplated the divine possibilities that lay within human nature. He bubbled with optimism as he perceived the eventual triumph of God in the hearts of people and in the creation. In a sermon before the Yearly Meeting of Progressive Friends in Longwood, Pennsylvania, on May 31, 1858, Parker exalted as he spoke of the joy a person could experience in God. "If a man be sure of the Infinite Perfection of God," the preacher assured, "what tranquility and delight is there for him." After enumerating some of the great joys he had experienced in life, Parker proclaimed, "But I must confess that the chiefest of all my delights is still the religious." He shared with his listeners what God had meant in his life.

What delight have I in my consciousness of God, the certainty of his protection, of his Infinite Love! There is an Infinite Father—nay, Infinite Mother is the dearer and more precious name—who takes a special care of me, and has made this world, with its vast forces, to serve and bless me.

Parker said that such a joyous experience of God was available to every person, regardless of label or sect. "Do not think that God knows only such as 'know Christ,' or Moses," he certified. "He is no respecter of persons. The footsteps of religion . . . are deeply set in the primeval rock of history. How multitudinous are the conceptions of God, all meant to satisfy the soul which longs for Him!"[136]

In another sermon, Parker was rapturous as he contemplated the beauties and wonders of nature.

Even animals we think austere and sad, the lonely hawk, the solitary jay, who loves New England winters, and the innumerable shellfish, have their personal and domestic joy. The toad whom we vilify as ugly and even call venomous, malicious, and spiteful, is a kind neighbor and seems as contented as the day is long. So it is with the spider who is not the malignant kidnapper that he is thought, but has a little harmless world of joy. . . . Go into the fields, at morning, noon, or night, and all creation is a-hum with happiness, the young and old, the reptile, insect, beast, and fowls of heaven rejoice in their brave delight. All about us is full of joy, fuller than we notice. Take a handful of water from the rotting timbers of a wharf; little polyps are therein, medusae and the like, with few senses, few faculties; but they all swim in a tide of joy, and it seems as if the world was made for them alone.[137]

Parker's public prayers, almost without exception, radiated a deep sense of serenity and trust, a profound gratitude, and optimistic faith. Even on those Sundays when the sermon appeared harsh in nature, a very different spirit and mood permeated his prayers. The following is a portion of a Sunday morning pastoral prayer offered at the beginning of a new year. The prayer is a prototype of most of Parker's public prayers.

O thou Infinite Spirit, we thank thee for all thy loving-kindness and thy tender mercy, which gave us our being first, and lengthenest out our lives from day to day, and from year to year, while thou presentest before us the immortal life, which eye has not seen, nor ear heard, nor our frail hearts completely understood.

We thank thee for this fair sunlight which gladdens and cheers the faces of men, while it fills up with handsomeness the wintry hour. We thank thee for the stars, which all night long keep shining watch above a sleeping world; and we bless thee for thy providence, which cares for us when we slumber, and when we wake. Yes, we thank thee that underneath thy care we can lay us down and sleep in safety, and when we wake we are still with thee.

While we stand at the entrance of a new year, remembering thy presence with us, we cast our eyes backward, and we thank thee for all the joy and gladness which came to our lot in the months that are past. We thank thee for the health and energy that have been in our earthly frame. We bless thee for the work our hands found to do, for the joy which comes from the harvested result of our toil and thought, and that greater but unasked joy and blessedness which comes from the education which the process of our daily toil in thy marvelous providence doth bring about.[138]

Louisa M. Alcott wrote of the first time she heard Parker preach. She thought the sermon had been especially designed for her. "To one laborious young woman, just setting forth to seek her fortune," Alcott testified, "that Sunday was the beginning of a new life, that sermon like the scroll given to Christian . . . a valiant Great-heart leading pilgrims through Vanity Fair to the Celestial City." But it was Parker's prayer that made the deepest impression upon that particular listener.

But the prayer that followed went straight to the hearts of those for whom he prayed,—not only comforting by its tenderness, and strengthening by its brave and cheerful spirit, but showing them where to go for greater help, and how to ask it as simply and confidingly as he did.

It was unlike any prayer I had ever heard; not cold and formal, as if uttered from a sense of duty, not a display of eloquence, nor an impious directing of Deity in his duties toward humanity. It was a quiet talk with God, as if long intercourse and much love had made it natural and easy for the son to seek the Father,—confessing faults, asking help, and submitting all things to the All-wise and tender, as freely as children bring their little sorrows, hopes and fears to their mother's knee.

The slow, soft folding of the hands, the reverent bowing of the good gray head, the tears that sometimes veiled the voice, the simplicity, frankness, and devout earnestness, made both words and manner wonderfully eloquent; and the phrase, "Our Father and our Mother God," was inexpressibly sweet and beautiful,—seeming to invoke both power and love to sustain and comfort the anxious, overburdened hearts of those who listened and went away to labor and to wait with fresh hope and faith.[139]

Though Parker saw evil everywhere—in individuals, in all kinds of social institutions, even in the church—he was always optimistic that in the long run evil was a dead end street and that right would ultimately triumph. That was a part of his Christian faith, a belief in a loving and perfect God who would see his own nature fulfilled on earth even as it was in heaven. It was a part of his Transcendental faith, a belief in the divinity and perfectibility of man. It was a part of his American faith, a belief in progress that knew no bounds. Such faith enabled Parker to verbally lash out against the wrongs of his era, though that often meant offending wealthy and powerful interests. Such optimism supplied him with courage to challenge what often seemed to be unwinable odds. He was confident that even the greatest evil of them all, slavery, would some day be no more.

There was a temporal quality in Parker's sermons. His concern with the past was only as a source from which to draw lessons and examples to be applied to the present. He spoke of the failures of Boston rather than the delinquencies of Babylonia. His emphasis was upon contemporary America rather than ancient Assyria. He addressed the needs of the nineteenth century rather than the problems of the first century. Robert T. Oliver has noted that Parker "drew the substance for his preaching not from a study of the Bible nor of other books (although he was a voracious reader with a remarkable retentive memory) but from looking around him to see what needed to be set right."[140] Because his orations, especially his sermons, were so contemporary in their focus, it is difficult for people of another era to experience what those discourses meant to those who heard them. Because we are generations removed from the passion of those issues and ideas that absorbed people's hearts and minds in the mid-nineteenth century, it becomes extremely difficult to capture the effect of Parker's oratory.

Whereas most preachers in Parker's day, or any day for that matter, looked to the Bible, the Church, creeds or tradition as their sources of authority, Parker's source of authority was seldom found beyond his own intuition. McCall has noted that "in one volume of eleven representative sermons, for example, authority is used not once. Even the Bible, which is the ultimate source of authority for most ministers, he used for texts and inspiration but not for authoritative reference. Great religious teachers of the past he used more often as objects of criticism than as support of his statements."[141] Parker's criticism of various Church Fathers has already been noted. Other Church Fathers also received withering comments from his Boston pulpit.

Tertullian introduced more heresies and ridiculous doctrines into the Church than almost all the Fathers. . . . Origen was not a good Hebrew scholar. . . . Jerome loved glory rather than truth. . . . St. Augustine introduced more errors into the Church than any other man. . . . Chrysostom was better than most, but he was often absurd in his interpretations.[142]

It was not that Parker neglected previous scholarship, reasoning, history, or the inductive method. The reasoning process was used to support and confirm intuition, but not replace it as the basis for the knowing process. Such was Parker's approach to all knowing, even the knowing of God, where "belief always precedes the proof."

Our belief in God's existence does not depend on the *a posteriori* argument, or considerations drawn from the order, fitness and beauty discovered by observations made in the material world; nor yet on the *a priori* argument, on considerations drawn from the external nature of things, and observations made in the spiritual world. It depends primarily on *no argument* whatever, not on reasoning, but *Reason*. The fact is given outright, as it were, and comes to the man, as soon and as naturally, as the belief of his own existence. . . . This intuitive perception of God is afterwards fundamentally and logically established by the *a priori* argument, and beautifully confirmed by the *a posteriori* argument; but we are not left with the Idea of God till we become metaphysicians and naturalists and so can discover it by much thinking. It comes spontaneously, by a law of whose actions we are, at first, not conscious. The belief always precedes the proof; intuition gives the thing to be reasoned about. Unless the intuitive function be performed, it is not possible to attain a knowledge of God.[143]

Parker made frequent use of figures of speech, especially the metaphor, and mildly criticized himself for excessive use of this tool. In an 1841 Letter to Elizabeth Peabody, he observed: "In all my sermons is an excess of metaphors, similes, and all sorts of figures of speech. But this is my nature—I could not help it if I would." He drew his illustrations and analogies "from the common objects,"[144] and criticized noted preachers from the past for taking "their figures from the schoolmen," rather than from the common and ordinary objects of everyday life. "The writings of Taylor, or Barrow and South, of Bossuet, Massillon, and Bourdalove," declared Parker, "always presuppose a narrow audience of men of nice culture. So they draw their figures from the schoolmen, from the Greek anthology, from heathen classics and the Christian Fathers. Their illustrations were embellishments to the scholar, but only palpable darkness to the people."[145] Note some examples of Parker's use of various figures of speech.

Slavery, the most hideous snake which southern regions breed, with fifteen unequal feet, come crawling north; the avarice, the foulest worm which northern cities gender in their heart, went crawling south.[146]

Mr. Webster stamped his foot, and broke through into the great hallow of practical atheism. . . . The firm-set base of northern cities quaked and yawned with gaping rents. Penn's "Sandy foundation" shook again, and black men fled from the city of brotherly love, as doves, with plaintive cry, flee from a farmer's barn when summer lightning stabs the roof. There was a twist in Faneuil, and the doors could not open wide enough for Liberty to regain her ancient cradle.[147]

How noisy is this great channel of business, wherein humanity rolls to and fro, now running into shops, now sucked down into cellars.[148]

Parker's written manuscripts give little evidence of humor. In this regard the contrast with Henry Ward Beecher—who regaled his audiences with laughter—was greatly evident.[149] Parker looked upon such a technique as gimmickry, as did most clergymen of that era. However, Parker's addresses were not considered dour and his audiences testified as to appreciating his wit. For Parker, there were "no tricks in real eloquence; [such tricks] belong . . . only to the low practice of the stage. . . . An impressive mode of delivery . . . will depend on qualities that lie a good deal deeper than the surface." For Parker it was important for the speaker to be natural in his delivery. "Nature is the guide," he emphasized. It was important, Parker declared, that the orator "speak distinctly and in the natural tones of conversation as far as possible."[150] There was neither artificiality nor ostentation in Parker's manner of oratory.

If there was nothing dramatically unique in Parker's oratorical style, neither was there anything particularly special in his oratorical appearance. Oliver has observed that "Parker was far from being oratorical in appearance or manner. He stood five feet eight inches, was early bald, and by the age of forty had a snow-white beard. His features were plain, his gestures few and graceless, and he read all his sermons."[151] Yet, Parker mesmerized his audiences. His sermons and other orations were lengthy by contemporary standards—almost always an hour and often much longer. Nevertheless, we are told, his audiences stayed focused on the speaker and his words until he had completed what he had to say. Octavius Brooks Frothingham, a noted Unitarian clergyman, who heard Parker on many occasions, observed that Parker "had no rhetorical gifts. . . . Neither was his figure imposing, nor his gestures fine, nor his actions graceful." Yet, Frothingham continued, "the style was never dry; the words were sinewy; the sentences short and pithy; the language was fragrant with the odor of the fields, and rich with the juices of the ground, passages of exquisite beauty bloomed on every page."[152]

Twenty years after Parker's death, an aging Ralph Waldo Emerson was reflecting in a speech on some of those he had known throughout his life. He remembered Theodore Parker, the orator, as one who "was no artist," but who, nevertheless, spoke with an "element of beauty."

Theodore Parker was our Savonarola, an excellent scholar, in frank and affectionate communication with the best minds of his day, yet the tribune of the people, and the stout Reformer to urge and defend every cause of humanity with and for the humblest of mankind. He was no artist. Highly refined persons might easily miss in him the element of beauty. What he said was mere fact, almost offended you, so bald and detached; little cared he. He stood together for practical truth; and so to the last. He used every day and hour of his short life, and his character appeared in the last moments with the same firm control as in the midday of strength.[153]

James Russell Lowell, who heard several of Parker's orations, drew a poetic picture of the preacher that was quite in harmony with the observations of Frothingham and Emerson.

> There he stands looking more like a ploughman than a priest,
> If not dreadfully awkward, not graceful at least,
> His gestures all downright and same, if you will,
> As a brown-fisted Hobnail in hoeing a drill;
> But his periods fall on you, stroke after stroke,
> Like the blows of a lumberer felling an oak,
> You forget the man wholly, you're thankful to meet
> With a preacher who smacks of the field and the street.[154]

Oliver has written that "the principle sources of his [Parker's] power were that he thought independently, he said what he thought, and he personalized his messages so that they penetrated to every hearer."[155] There were many who were captivated not just by the power but by the poetic beauty of Parker's oratory. William Seward judged Parker's oratory as "beautiful, superbly beautiful." Charles Sumner—a man with whom Parker carried on a long correspondence—thought the words of Parker "like the music of Mozart."[156]

Parker's speeches influenced the thoughts and words of another great mid-nineteenth century orator, Abraham Lincoln. Though the two gifted speakers never met, there is ample evidence of Parker's influence upon Lincoln during the future president's days in Springfield, Illinois. Jesse Fell, a long-time Lincoln friend and associate, spoke of Parker's influence on Lincoln's religious thought. "If from my recollections on this subject [religion]," noted Fell, "I was called upon to designate an author whose views most nearly represent Mr. Lincoln's on this subject, I would say that author was Theodore Parker." Fell related that he believed Lincoln was not in harmony with all of Parker's views, "yet they were generally much admired and appreciated by him."[157] William Herndon, Lincoln's law partner in Springfield, wrote of bringing the words of Parker to Lincoln's attention. In 1858, upon returning from a trip to New England, Herndon reported:

I brought with me additional sermons and lectures by Theodore Parker, who was warm in his commendation of Lincoln. One of these was a lecture on "The Effect of Slavery on the American People" . . . which I gave to Lincoln, who read and returned it. He liked especially the following expression, which he marked with a pencil, and which he in substance afterwards used in his Gettysburg address: "Democracy is direct self-government, over all the people, for all the people, by all the people."[158]

On another occasion, Parker spoke of "democracy—as government of all, for all, and by all."[159] Garry Wills has noted that these "words bring to mind the point on which most historians grant Parker's influence on Lincoln. The great preacher constantly used a triple refrain describing government of, by, and for the people. Herndon was certain that Lincoln read one such formulation, and there were many of them scattered through Parker's writings."[160]

It has already been noted that there was yet another famous phrase that Abraham Lincoln may have borrowed from Parker. On May 18, 1858, Lincoln, in a speech at Edwardsville, Illinois, used for the first time, of which there is a record, the "house-divided" metaphor, although he said he had alluded to it a year before. In the Edwardsville speech, Lincoln predicted: "'A house divided against itself cannot stand.' I believe the government cannot endure permanently half slave and half free. I expressed this belief a year ago."[161] James M. McPherson has written that "this metaphor of a house divided became probably the single most important image of the relationship between slavery and the Union, and remains so today. It provided an instant mental picture of what Republicans stood for."[162] Lincoln repeated the metaphor (found in all three synoptic gospels: Matthew 12:25, Mark 3:25, Luke 11:17) one month later on June 16 at the Republican state convention in Springfield, and again in an address on September 16, 1859, in Columbus, Ohio. However, at least three years before Lincoln first applied this biblical text to the national dilemma, Theodore Parker, on July 11, 1854, had drawn a similar application. "There can be no national welfare," Parker affirmed, "without a national unity of action. That cannot take place unless there is a national Unity of Idea in fundamentals. Without this a nation is a 'house divided against itself,' of course, it cannot stand."[163] It can only be speculated as to whether Lincoln was influenced by Parker in the use of this dramatic metaphor. Most who have written on the subject think it highly likely.

A twentieth-century orator—Martin Luther King Jr.—also borrowed from Theodore Parker. One of King's favorite lines was: "The arc of the moral universe is long, but it bends toward justice." This cautiously optimistic phrase is an exact quotation from Parker. Like Lincoln before him, King never credited the original source.[164]

That which most compelled the attention of Parker's listeners were qualities within the orator himself; his inner integrity, his moral passion, his obvious sincerity, and his vast learning which he organized and presented in a manner the common man could appreciate and understand. Parker stood as a prime example of Aristotle's teaching that ethical proof—the character of the speaker—is "the most potent of all the means of persuasion."[165] John Weiss recalled that "the most impressive thing in Boston on those Sundays [when Parker preached] was the moral sincerity of the preacher's voice, as it deepened from common sense to religious emotion, or sparkled into indignation that was not for sale, or softened into sympathy and human pleasure at the Beautiful and the Good."[166] Nearly a quarter of a century after Parker's death, the Lord Chief Justice of England, John

Duke Coleridge, in an 1883 speech at Boston, was loudly applauded when he referred to Parker as "perhaps one of your highest and greatest souls."[167] The following year, James Russell Lowell spoke in England, and praised the memory of Parker for teaching that "Democracy meant not 'I'm as good as you are,' but 'you're as good as I am.'"[168]

4

The Waning Months (1859–1860)

In the spring of 1857, Theodore Parker was miserably sick. For the past few years consumption had plagued his body. He would slow down for brief periods, enough to regain some of his strength, and then continued on with his rigorous schedule. His congregation had noted the debilitating effects and urged their pastor to take an extended paid leave of absence. The preacher allowed himself a few days off, but it had never been his nature to be idle for long. There was too much to be done and so much more to say. Even in the spring of 1857, he slowed only for short periods, and then it was back to the lecture circuit, sermons at the Music Hall, and other responsibilities.

A friend noted what was happening. "Mr. Parker works day and night. He is doing the work of half a dozen men. He is burning the candle at both ends. . . . He is only in his forty-seventh year. . . . But when I see him in the pulpit, oh, how much older he looks! His head is bald and his beard white, or almost so. He is giving his life to his work in a terrible sense." Parker himself wrote in that year of 1857: "I am forty-seven by the reckoning of my mother, seventy-four by my own internal account. I am an old man."[1]

As the new year began in 1859, Parker's health had deteriorated to the point where even he admitted to himself that his time might be short. On January 1, he wrote in his journal:

This is the first New Year's Day that I was ever sick. Now I have been a prisoner almost three months, living in my chamber or my study. The doctor says I mend, and I quote him to my friends. But I have great doubts as to the results. It looks as if this was the last of my New Year's days on earth. I felt so when I gave each gift to-day; yet few men have more to live for than I. It seems as if I had just begun a great work.[2]

The next day, Sunday, January 2, Parker delivered a sermon titled, "What

Religion May Do For a Man." It was a strenuous effort. The preacher leaned
heavily upon the pulpit, gripping it tightly with his hands. It was the last sermon
he would ever preach. The following Sunday, the congregation thronged the
sanctuary. They came to hear another one of those wonderful sermons, but they
also came out of concern for their pastor's obviously failing health. The familiar
figure did not come. Instead, a deacon read to them a note from Parker.

Well-beloved friends, I shall not speak to you today; for this morning a little after four
o'clock I had a slight attack of bleeding from the lungs or throat. I intended to preach on
"The Religion of Jesus and the Christianity of the Church," or "The Superiority of Good-
Will to Man over Theological Fancies."
   I hope you will not forget the contribution for the poor whom we have with us
always. I don't know when I shall again look upon your welcome faces, which have so
often cheered my spirit when my flesh was weak.
   May we do justly, love mercy, and walk humbly with our God, and his blessing will
be upon us here and hereafter, for his infinite love is with us forever and ever.[3]

The Twenty-Eighth Congregational Society immediately voted at least a
year's leave of absence with full pay for Parker. During that time he was to
devote himself solely to the restoration of his health. On January 23, Parker's
physician informed the patient that his chances of recovery were one in ten. That
night, Parker recorded his thoughts on the diagnosis. He was not afraid of death,
but there was so much more to do, and he hoped to beat the odds.

When I see the Inevitable, I fall in love with her. To die will be no evil to me. I should
like to finish my work, write up my hints, print my best sermons, finish my book, write
my autobiography, with sketches of my acquaintances, put all my papers in order. Yet I
am ready. But I mean to live, and not die. I laugh at the odds of nine to one. If that is all,
I'll conquer. I have fought ninety-nine against one, 999 against one, and conquered. Please
God, I will again.[4]

Letters of concern and support came from all over America and various parts
of the world. Parker spent much of his time replying to those letters and
writing—sometimes very long letters—to those who had played an important role
in his life. William Lloyd Garrison wrote to Parker, and the minister wrote back:

Three men now living have done New England and the North great service, . . . all
soldiers in the same great cause, William L. Garrison, Horace Mann, and R. W. Emerson.
You took the most dangerous and difficult part, and no soldier ever fought with more
gallant hardihood, no martyr ever more nobly bore what came as the earthly reward of
his nobleness. . . . I value Integrity above all human virtues. I never knew yours to
fail—no, nor even falter. God bless you for it![5]

Doctors and friends insisted that Parker leave for a more favorable climate
than Boston. It was his only chance. On February 8, Parker, Lydia, and a few
friends set sail for Santa Cruz. Aboard ship, Parker began a book-length letter

to his congregation that would be titled, *Theodore Parker's Experience As A Minister*. The manuscript, 40,000 words in length, was finished in Santa Cruz on April 19 and sent off to the beloved members of the Twenty-Eighth Congregational Society. The letter was later printed as a book and stands as the best single source of Parker's estimation of himself and the work he accomplished. He had hoped to follow with an autobiography, but failing health determined that only a few pages of that autobiography would be written.

In *Experience As A Minister* Parker revealed that he was continually thinking about sermons he would like to preach. "Sermons are never out of my mind," he wrote. Observing the beauties of the Caribbean, he mused,

all these common things turn into poetry as I look on or am compelled to hear, and then transfigure into sermons, which come also spontaneously by night and give themselves to me, and even in my sleep they are meant for you. Shall they ever be more than the walking of

a sick man in his sleep,
Three paces and then faltering?[6]

He also reviewed the various subjects on which he had already preached.

I have preached much on the great Social Duties of your time and place. . . . I have preached against Intemperance, showing the monstrous evil of drunkenness. . . . I have preached against covetousness—the abnormal desire of accumulating property. . . . I have spoken of the tyranny of the rich over the thriving and the poor. . . . I have preached much on the condition of women. . . . I have preached against war. . . . I have spoken against slavery more than any other concrete wrong, because it is the greatest of all, "the sum, of all villainies.". . . I have preached against the Errors of the Ecclesiastical Theology . . . for they are the most fatal mischiefs in the land.[7]

On June 1, Parker and his traveling companions arrived in London, Parker noting that he was "too feeble to do much."[8] On June 12 he was in Paris and ten days later in Switzerland. At each stop along the way, friends from Europe and the United States came to greet and visit with this much-admired clergyman from Boston. Such visits were sometimes difficult for a man as sick as Parker, but they also infused him with renewed strength and purpose. On July 27, Parker arrived at the mountain chalet of his dear friend, Edward De Sor. Here he would stay for several weeks and began to show signs of dramatic physical improvement. He gained weight. He chopped wood. He wrote a paper on "The Bumblebee's Thoughts on the Plan and Purpose of the Universe." He received a steady stream of visitors and spent long hours writing letters. One letter was to the Twenty-Eighth Congregational Society in which Parker tendered his resignation. The congregation refused to accept it, preferring to regard Parker as their pastor and leader as long as he lived. Though he understood such sentiments, Parker was concerned about a flock of sheep that had no shepherd.[9]

Yet, Parker was encouraged by the physical progress he was making during his summer stay in the mountains.

With the coming of autumn the mountains became too cold a place for a frail body. Therefore, on October 21, Parker and his companions moved south to Rome. Unfortunately, Rome that season was unusually cold and damp and Parker's health took a turn for the worse. He, nevertheless, continued to be as involved as possible. He participated in archeological excavations and enjoyed the various sights of the ancient city. Numerous friends continued to stop by: Hawthorne, Bryant, Harriet Beecher Stowe, the Brownings, and so many others. Visitors continued to be a tonic for a man who knew that he was steadily losing his strength.

There was so much about Rome that Parker disliked. In a letter to George Ripley, on October 29, Parker wrote of his distaste for the pageantry of the Catholic Church. "What a heathenish place it is," he complained. "The Roman religion is addressed to the senses, and must, ere long, go the same road as the Egyptian religion, and its successors. Protestantism will in due time follow, it being a little less absurd than Catholicism." Parker even failed to be impressed with the art of Rome. "The fine arts do not impress me so much as the course arts, which feed, clothe, house, and comfort people," he affirmed. "I should rather be such a great man as Franklin than a Michaelangelo." Parker also expressed his skepticism of Roman literary and intellectual pursuits. There was one thing he did appreciate in Rome. "The Italian women are generally handsome," he wrote. "In America, as in France, Germany, and Switzerland, the homely women are in the majority . . . here they are in the small minority. The Lord be praised for his mercies!" He wrote of how he planned to spend his time in Rome.

Here I am booked for six months—if I live so long—having paid my board for that time. I have a deal of work to do, as follows:—(1) to study the geology of Rome; (2) its flora and fauna; (3) its archaeology; (4) its architecture. I have begun already, though I have been here but a few days. This work will keep me out of doors all the pleasant weather, and turn my mind off from myself, one of the most disagreeable subjects of contemplation.[10]

It was at Rome that Parker heard of John Brown's raid on Harper's Ferry, his capture and trial, and his impending execution on December 2. On November 24, in a letter to Frances Jackson, Parker expressed his personal sentiments on John Brown and his actions.

Brown will die, I think, like a martyr, and also like a saint. His noble demeanor, his unflinching bravery, his gentleness, his calm, religious trust in God, and his words of truth and soberness, cannot fail to make a profound impression on the hearts of Northern men; yes, and on Southern men. . . . Let the American State hang his body, and the American Church damn his soul; still, the blessings of such as are ready to perish will fall on him, and the universal justice of the Infinitely Perfect God will take him welcome home. The road to heaven is as short from the gallows as from the throne; perhaps, also, as easy.[11]

With the coming of the new year, there seemed to be a marked decline in Parker's health. In a letter, dated January 16, 1860, Parker's friend, Robert Apthorp, wrote of his observations as to Parker's condition: " . . . a constant diminution of vitality. . . . He is, I think, ten or twelve pounds lighter, more nervous and desponding, thinner in the face, complexion paler, eyes much feebler-looking, having lost a great deal of their fire and expression."[12] In mid-April, Parker, much aware that the end could be near, demanded to leave Rome for Florence. Friends tried to dissuade him, fearing that he would die enroute. With great determination, Parker—who was seldom denied—responded: "I will not die here, I will not leave my bones in this detested soil; I will go to Florence and I will get there—that I promise you."[13]

On April 22, Parker and his party left Rome, leaving behind the great dome of St. Peter's, which for Parker was a foreboding symbol of ecclesiastical tyranny. The one hundred and fifty mile journey to Florence was made in five days. Parker rode in a specially prepared carriage. He asked to be told when they passed beyond the boundaries of the papal states, and when informed, "he roused as if electrified."[14] In Florence, he met for the first time, Frances Power Cobbe, with whom he had corresponded for years, and who in the not too distant future would edit and publish Parker's papers. To Miss Cobbe, Parker noted, "I have had great powers and have only half used them." Later, perhaps in confusion, perhaps in vindication, he said to her: "There are two Theodore Parkers now: one is dying here in Italy; the other I have planted in America. He will live there and finish my work."[15]

On Thursday, May 10, 1860, Theodore Parker died. In August he would have celebrated his fiftieth birthday. He had steadily weakened but there had been no apparent suffering. The end came so quickly and quietly that it was difficult to know the moment of death. The following Sunday his body was buried in the Protestant cemetery, just beyond the city limits of Florence. A relatively simple stone marked the place of burial, inscribed with even more simple words of Parker's own choosing.

THEODORE PARKER
Born at Lexington, Mass.,
United States of America
Aug. 24, 1810
Died at Florence, May 10, 1860

At Parker's memorial service in Boston, Emerson proclaimed:

Ah, my brave brother! It seems as if, in a frivolous age, our loss was immense, and your place cannot be supplied. But you will already be consoled in the transfer of your genius, knowing well that the nature of the world will affirm to all men, in all times, that which for twenty-five years you valiantly spoke. The breezes of Italy murmur the same truth over your grave, the winds of America over these bereaved streets, and the sea which bore your mourners home affirms it. Whilst the polished and pleasant traitors to human rights, with perverted learning and disgraced grace, die and are utterly forgotten, with their double tongue saying all that is sordid about the corruption of man, you believed in the divinity of all, and you live on.[16]

In the fall of 1866, Frederick Douglass, a former slave, and himself a great orator, visited Parker's grave. Standing by the headstone, Douglass recalled "the many services rendered the cause of human freedom by him [Parker], freedom not only from physical chains but the chains of superstition, those which not only galled the limbs and tore the flesh, but those which marred and wounded the human soul." Douglass remembered that Parker "had a voice for the slave; when nearly all the pulpits in the land were dumb."[17]

On Thanksgiving Day, 1891, a new monument was dedicated at Parker's grave. It was more elaborate than the first. Parker's face was etched in the stone encircled by a laurel wreath. Following Parker's name, the words, "The Great American Preacher" were added. The final words on the monument read: "His name is engraved in marble, his virtues in the hearts of those he helped to free from slavery and superstition."[18]

PART II

SERMONS AND SPEECHES OF THEODORE PARKER

Part II consists of three Parker sermons/speeches, printed in their entirety. The three discourses originate from Parker's "Years of Influence (1841–1859)." Each speech will be preceded by brief introductory remarks. The paragraphs of "A Sermon Of Slavery" (1841) are numbered to aid in a closer analysis of the speech. The following two speeches—"The Mexican War" (1849) and "The Revival Of Religion Which We Need" (1858)—are not as closely analyzed, but preceding remarks will point out important facets of those speeches and place them in their larger context.

"A SERMON OF SLAVERY" (1841)

Parker delivered "A Sermon of Slavery" in 1841, some twenty years before General Beauregard directed the bombardment against Fort Sumter. It was his first antislavery sermon. As was his custom, Parker clearly stated his theme early in the sermon. At the beginning of the third paragraph, Parker announced: "Now man was made to be free, to govern himself, to be his own master, to have no cause stand between him and God, which shall curtail his birthright of freedom." This specific ordering of words is not repeated again in the sermon, but the entire discourse is an elaboration and development of this theme.

The purpose of Parker's sermon is to persuade people to resist those obstacles which curtail human freedom, whether those obstacles were external or internal. In the conclusion of the sermon (¶s 23–28), Parker summons his listeners to action against both kinds of obstacles or slavery. In paragraph twenty-four he urges listeners to resist external or "bodily" slavery. He advocates disobedience of, and the rewriting of, human laws which are contrary to divine law. In paragraph twenty-five, Parker emphasized, "Bodily slavery, though established by the powers that be, is completely in the hands of the voters." As to internal slavery, he declared: "But that other slavery, which

comes from yourself, that is wholly within your power. . . . freedom for the
soul to act right, think right, feel right, you cannot inherit; that you must win
for yourself" (¶s 26, 28).

The arrangement of material held the highest priority in Parker's
construction of a sermon. Therefore, it is not surprising that the organization of
this sermon is clearly perceived. In his introduction (¶s 1–5) Parker first states
and then elaborates upon his theme that men were created to be free and should
allow nothing to obstruct that birthright of freedom. The first paragraph relates
that theme to a biblical text. The body of the discourse (¶s 6–22) contains two
divisions wherein Parker discusses those obstacles which restrict freedom. In the
first division (¶s 6–18), he spoke of external obstacles and presented a masterful
argument against the institution of slavery. In the second division (¶s 19–22),
Parker spoke against internal obstacles to freedom, those things people do to
themselves to restrict their own liberty. He directed his attack against the
mischiefs of the heart, and specified sins such as avarice, passion, peevishness,
and intemperance. In his conclusion (¶s 23–28), Parker summoned men to take
action against both kinds of hindrances to freedom.

Parker was a master in the use of logic to persuade. There are several
examples of this rhetorical tool in the sermon. In paragraphs eight through ten,
Parker sought to demolish the various arguments that some northerners proposed
to defend southern slavery. In paragraph seventeen he dealt with those in the
North who claimed that slavery was not a northern concern. These instances are
examples of classical refutation whereby the speaker seeks to demolish the
arguments of those with whom he disagrees. In paragraph eighteen, Parker
developed a compelling case for northern accommodation in the institution of
slavery. His arguments are clear, precise, and effectively ordered. His debating
skills are finely honed. Note his great care in defining terms such as "bodily
slavery" (¶ 2) and "freedom" (¶s 3–4).

Parker's illustrations are so carefully woven into the sermon that they often
fail to appear as illustrations. He cites the example of "a knave plundering a
little girl out of fortune" to portray what slavery has done to the African (¶ 7).
He pulls in an illustration from colonial America to defeat a northern argument
defending slavery (¶ 8). He recalls the example of Jesus to strengthen another
debating point (¶ 9). The abolitionists are used as examples of what a stand
against slavery should be, with Parker making a strong endorsement of the
abolitionists' motives and methods (¶ 15).

Parker's transitions between divisions of the sermon are smooth and
logical. Paragraphs four and five allow for a natural flow from the introduction
to the main body of the sermon. In like manner, the first sentence of paragraph
nineteen is a simple but orderly transition from the first division to the second
division.

The sermon is a prime example of Parker's ability to deal with "superior
ideas," and yet put those ideas into words and reasoning that most people of his
day could comprehend. Though there is careful logic in his development, one
senses, even on the printed page, a certain passion behind the words; a passion
in the heart and mind of the speaker, and a passion certainly noted by those
who heard him.

Parker's source of authority was his own intuition of divine right and wrong. For him, this was the higher law; a law that stood above the Constitution and the laws of the land (¶ 24). It was a law that stood even above the scriptures, for, as Parker noted, slave owners often used the scriptures to justify slavery (¶ 24). In the Bible, he argued, "a man finds what he looks for." As was his common practice, Parker used a biblical text as a starting point for his sermon, but not as a source of authority.

Parker's sermon reveals much about the era in which it was preached. It demonstrates that in 1841 the slavery issue was being passionately debated. It speaks of some northern attempts to justify slavery (¶s 8–10); of other northern justifications to look the other way on the issue (¶ 17); and of northern complicity in slavery (¶ 18). It tells about the kind of people in the North who failed to take a stand against slavery and what their motives might have been (¶s 12–13, 16–18). The sermon, in a few words, tells the reader about the abolitionists and how they were perceived at that time (¶ 15). "A Sermon of Slavery" is a valuable document which enlightens the reader as to the sectional crisis and debate on slavery twenty years before the Civil War began.

Know ye not that to whom ye yield yourselves servants to obey, his servants ye are whom ye obey; whether of sin unto death, or of obedience unto righteousness?
—Rom. VI. 16.

1   In our version of the New Testament, the word *servant* often stands for a word in the original, which means *slave*. Such is the case in this passage just read, and the sense of the whole verse is this:—"If a man yields unconditional service to sin, he is the *slave* of sin, and gets death for his reward." Here, however, by a curious figure of speech, not uncommon in this apostle, he uses the word *slave* in a good sense—*slave* of obedience unto righteousness. I now ask your attention to a short sermon of slavery.

2   A popular definition has sometimes been given of common bodily slavery, that it is the holding of property in man. In a kindred language it is called body-property. In this case a man's body becomes the possession, property, chattel, tool, or thing of another person, and not of the man who lives in it. This foreign person, of course, makes use of it to serve his own ends, without regard to the true welfare, or even the wishes, of the man who lives in that body, and to whom it rightfully belongs. Here the relation is necessarily that of force on one side and suffering on the other, though the force is often modified and the suffering sometimes disguised or kept out of sight.

3   Now man was made to be free, to govern himself, to be his own master, to have no cause stand between him and God, which shall curtail his birthright of freedom. He is never in his proper element until he attains this condition of freedom; of self-government. Of course, while we are children, not having reached the age of discretion, we must be under the authority of our parents and guardians, teachers, and friends. This is natural relation. There is no slavery in it; no degradation. The parents, exercising rightful authority over their children, do not represent human caprice, but divine wisdom and love. They assume the

direction of the child's actions, not to do themselves a service, but to benefit him. The father restrains his child, that the child may have more freedom, not less. Here the relation is not of force and suffering, but of love on both sides; of ability, which loves to help, and necessity, which loves to be directed. The child that is nurtured by its parent gains more than the parent does. So is it the duty of the wise, the good, the holy, to teach, direct, restrain the foolish, the wicked, the ungodly. If a man is wiser, better, and holier than I am, it is my duty, my privilege, my exaltation to obey him. For him to direct me in wisdom and love, not for his sake but for my own, is for me to be free. He may gain nothing by this, but I gain much.

4   As slavery was defined to be holding property in man, so freedom may be defined as a state in which the man does of his own consent, the best things he is capable of doing at that stage of his growth. Now there are two sorts of obstacles which prevent, or may prevent, man from attaining to this enviable condition of freedom. These are:—

I.   Obstacles external to ourselves, which restrict our freedom; and

II.   Obstacles internal to ourselves, which restrict our freedom.

5   A few words may be said on the condition to which men are brought by each of these classes of objects.

6   I.   Of the slavery which arises from a cause external to ourselves. By the blessing of Providence, seconding the efforts, prayers, tears of some good men, there is no bodily, personal slavery sanctioned by the law amongst us in New England. But at the South we all know that some millions of our fellow-citizens are held in bondage; that men, women, and children are bought and sold in the shambles of the national capital; are owned as cattle; reared as cattle; beaten as cattle. We all know that our fathers fought through the War of Independence with these maxims in their mouths and blazoned on their banners: that all men are born free and equal, and that the God of eternal justice will at last avenge the cause of the oppressed, however strong the oppressor may be; yet it is just as well known that the sons of those very fathers now trade in human flesh, separating parent and child, and husband and wife, for the sake of a little gain; that the sons of those fathers eat bread not in the sweat of their own brow, but in that of the slave's face; that they are sustained, educated, rendered rich, and haughty, and luxurious by the labor they extort from men whom they have stolen, or purchased from the stealer, or inherited from the purchaser. It is known to you all, that there are some millions of these forlorn children of Adam, men whom the Declaration of Independence declares "born free and equal" with their master before God and the Law; men whom the Bible names "of the same blood" with the prophets and apostles; men "for whom Christ died," and who are "statues of God in ebony"—that they are held in this condition and made to feel the full burden of a corrupt society, and doomed from their birth to degradation and infamy, their very name a mock-word; their life a retreat not a prog-ress,—for the general and natural effect of slavery is to lessen the qualities of a man in the slave as he increases in stature or in years,—their children, their

wives, their own bones and sinews at the mercy of a master! That these things are so, is known to all of us; well known from our childhood.

7   Every man who has ever thought at all on any subject, and has at the same time a particle of manhood in him, knows that this state of slavery would be to him worse than a thousand deaths; that set death in one scale, and hopeless slavery for himself and children in the other, he would not hesitate in his choice, but would say, "Give me death, though the life be ground out of me with the most exquisite fortunes of lingering agony that malice can invent or tyranny inflict." To the African thus made the victim of American cupidity and crime, the state of slavery, it will be said, may not appear so degrading as to you and me, for he has never before been civilized, and though the untaught instinct of man bid him love freedom, yet Christianity has not revealed to him the truth, that all men are brothers before God, born with equal rights. But this fact is no excuse for extenuation of our crime. Who would justify a knave in plundering a little girl out of a fortune that she inherited, on the ground that she was a little girl "of tender years," and had never enjoyed or even beheld her birthright? The fact, that the injured party was ignorant and weak, would only enhance and aggravate the offense, adding new baseness and the suspicion of cowardice to guilt. If the African be so low, that the condition of slavery is tolerable in his eyes, and he can dance in his chains—happy in the absence of the whip—it is all the more a sin, in the cultivated and the strong, in the Christian(!) to tyrannize over the feeble and defenseless. Men at the South with the Bible in one hand—with the Declaration of Independence in the other hand—with the word of Jesus, "Love your neighbor as yourself," pealing upon them from all quarters, attempt to justify slavery; not to excuse, to cloak, or conceal the thing, but to vindicate and defend it. This attempt, when made by reflecting men in their cool moments, discovers a greater degree of blackness of heart than the kidnapping of men itself. It is premeditated wickedness grown conscious of itself. The plain truth of the matter is this:—Men who wish for wealth and luxury, but hate the toil and sweat, which are their natural price, brought the African to America; they make his chains; they live by his tears; they dance to the piping of his groans; they fatten on his sweat and are pampered by his blood. If these men spoke as plainly as they must needs think, they would say openly; "our sin fettered them in slavery; and, please, God, our sin shall keep them in slavery till the world ends." This has been thought long enough, it is high time it was said also, that we may know what we are about and where we stand.

8   Men at the North sometimes attempt to gloss the matter over, and hush it up by saying the least possible on the subject. They tell us that some masters are "excellent Christians." No doubt it is so, estimating these masters by the common run of Christians,—you find such on the deck of pirate ships; in the dens of robbers. But suppose some slave holders are as good Christians as Fenelon or St. Peter; still a sin is a sin, though a Christian commit it. Our fathers did not think "taxation without representation" any the less an evil because imposed by "his most Christian Majesty," a King of Christians.

9   Then, too, it is said, "the slaves are very happy, and it is a great pity to disturb them," that "the whole mass are better fed and clothed, and are troubled with fewer cares, than working men at the North." Suppose this true also, what then? Do you estimate your welfare in pounds of beef; in yards of cloth; in exemption from the cares of a man! If so all appeal to you is vain, your own soul has become servile. The Saviour of the world was worse fed and clothed, no doubt, than many a Georgian slave, and had not where to lay his head, wearied with many cares; but has your Christianity taught you that was an evil, and the slave's hutch at night, and pottage by day, and exemption from a man's cares by night and day, are a good, a good to be weighed against freedom! Then are you unworthy of the soil you stand on; you contaminate the air of New England, which free men died to transmit to their children free!

10   Still further it is said, "the sufferings of slaves are often exaggerated." This may be true. No doubt there have been exaggerations of particular cases. Every slave-owner is not a demon, not a base man. No doubt there are what are called good Christians, men that would be ornaments to a Christian church, among slaveholders. But though there have been exaggerations in details, yet the awful sum of misery, unspeakable wretchedness, which hangs over two millions of slaves is such that eye hath not seen it; nor ear heard it; nor heart conceived of it. It were so if all their masters were Christians in character, in action, still retaining slaves. How much deeper and wilder must swell that wide weltering sea of human agony, when the masters are what we know so many are, hard-hearted and rapacious, insolent and brutal!

11   This attempt to gloss the matter over and veil the fact, comes from two classes of men.

12   1.   Some make the attempt from a real design to promote peace. They see no way to abate this mischief; they see "the folly and extravagance" of such as propose "dangerous measures," and therefore they would have us say nothing about it. The writhing patient is very sick; the leech more venturesome than skillful; and the friends, fearful to try the remedy, unwilling to summon wiser advice, declare the sick man is well as ever if you will only let him alone! These men mourn that any one should hold another in bondage; they think our fathers were illustrious heroes, for fighting dreadful wars with the parent country rather than pay a little tax against their will, but that this evil of slavery can never be healed; therefore, in the benevolence of their heart, they refuse to believe all the stories of suffering that reach their ears. The imagination of a kind man recoils at the thought of so much wretchedness; still more, if convinced that it cannot be abated. Now these men are governed by the best of motives, but it does not follow that their opinions are so just as their motives are good.

13   2.   But there are others, who are willing to countenance the sin and continue it, well knowing that it is a sin. They would not have it abated. They tell you of the stupidity of the African; that he is made for nothing but a slave; is allied to the baboon and the ape, and is as much in his place when fettered, ignorant and savage, in a rice field, to toil under a taskmaster's whip, as a New

Englander, free and educated, is in his place, when felling forests, planning railroads, or "conducting" a steam-engine. Hard treatment and poor fare, say they, are the black man's due. Besides, they add, there is a natural antipathy between the black race and the white, which only the love of money, or the love of power, on the part of the white is capable of overcoming; that the blacks are an inferior race, and therefore the white Saxons are justified in making them slaves. They think the strong have a right to the services of the weak, forgetting that the rule of reason, the rule of Christianity, is just the other way; "We that are strong ought to bear the infirmities of the weak." They would have us follow the old rule, "that they should get who have the power, and they should keep who can." Of this class nothing further need be said save this: that they are very numerous and quote the New Testament in support of slavery, thus contriving to pass for Christians, and have made such a stir in the land that it is scarce safe to open one's mouth and strip the veil from off this sin. . . .

14 The opinion of good and religious men here amongst us seems to be, that slavery is a great sin and ought to be abolished as soon as possible; that the talent and piety of the nation cannot be better employed than in devising the speediest and most effectual way of exterminating the evil. Such of them as see a way to abolish the wrong cry aloud and publish the tidings; others who see no way state that fact also, not failing to express their dread of all violent measures. Such is the conviction of good and religious men at the North. But there is another opinion a little different, which is held by a different class of men at the North;—they think that slavery is a great sin, and ought to be kept up so long as men can make money by it. But if the suppression of slavery could be effected—not as our fathers won their freedom, by blood and war—so gently as not to ruffle a sleeping baby's eyelid, yet if it diminished the crop of rice, or cotton, or tobacco, or corn, a single quintal a year, it would be a great mistake to free, cultivate, Christianize, and bless these millions of men! No one, I take it, will doubt this is a quite common opinion here in New England. The cause of this opinion will presently be touched upon. To show what baseness was implied in holding such opinions, would be simply a waste of time.

15 We all know there is at the North a small body of men, called by various names, and treated with various marks of disrespect, who are zealously striving to procure the liberation of slaves, in a peaceable and quiet way. They are willing to make any sacrifice for this end. They start from the maxim, that slavery is sin, and that sin is to be abandoned at once, and for ever, come what will come of it. These men, it is said, are sometimes extravagant in their speech; they do not treat the "patriarchal institution" with becoming reverence; they call slave-holders hard names, and appeal to all who have a heart in their bosoms, and to some who find none there, to join them and end the patriarchal institution by wise and Christian measures. What wonder is it that these men sometimes grow warm in their arguments! What wonder that their heart burns when they think of so many women exposed to contamination and nameless abuse; of so many children reared like beasts, and sold as oxen; of so many men owning no

property in their hands, or their feet, their hearts, or their lives! The wonder is all the other side, that they do not go to further extremities, sinful as it might be, and like St. John in his youth, pray for fire to come down from heaven and burn up the sinners, or like Paul, when he had not the excuse of youthful blood, ask God to curse them. Yet they do none of these things; never think of an appeal to the strong arm, but the Christian heart. . . . There is no doubt that these men are sometimes extravagant! There need be no wonder at that fact. The best of men have their infirmities, but if this extravagance be one of them, what shall we call the deadness of so many more amongst us? An infirmity? What shall we say of the sin itself? An infirmity also? Honest souls engaged in a good work, fired with a great idea, sometimes forget the settled decorum of speech, commonly observed in forum and pulpit, and call sin SIN. If the New Testament tell truth, Paul did so, and it was thought he would "turn the world upside down," while he was only striving to set it right. John the Baptist and Jesus of Nazareth did the same thing, and though one left his head in a charger, and the other his body on a cross, yet the world thinks at this day they did God's great work with their sincerity of speech.

16   The men who move in this matter encounter opposition from two classes of men; from the moderate, who do not see the wisdom of their measures, and who fear that the slave if set free will be worse off than before, or who think that the welfare of the masters is not sufficiently cared for. These moderate men think "we had better not meddle with the matter at present," but by and by, at a convenient season, they will venture to look into it. . . . Then too they encounter opposition from the selfish, who see, or think they see, that the white masters will lose some thousands of millions of dollars, if slavery be abolished! Who has forgotten the men that opposed the introduction of Christianity at Ephesus,—the craftsmen that made silver shrines for Diana!

17   I know some men say, "we have nothing to do with it. Slavery is the affair of the slave-owners and the slaves, not yours and mine. Let them abate it when they will." A most unchristian saying is this. Slavery! we have something to do with it. The sugar and rice we eat, the cotton we wear, are the work of the slave. His wrongs are imported to us in these things. We eat his flesh and drink his blood. I need not speak of our political connection with slavery. You all know what that is, and its effect on us here. But socially, individually, we are brought into contact with it every day. If there is a crime in the land known to us, and we do not protest against it to the extent of our ability, we are partners of that crime. It is not many years since it was said, temperate men had nothing to do with the sin of drunkenness; though they paid for it out of their purse! When they looked they found they had much to do with it, and sought to end it. . . .

18   Such then is slavery at the South; such the action of men at the North to attack or to defend it. But look a moment at the cause of this sin, and of its defense. It comes from the desire to get gain, comfort, or luxury; to have power over matter, without working or paying the honest price of that gain, comfort, luxury, and power; it is the spirit which would knowingly and of set purpose

injure another for the sake of gaining some benefit to yourself. Such a spirit would hold slaves everywhere, if it were possible. Now when the question is put to any fair man,—Is not this spirit active at the North as well as the South? there is but one answer. The man who would use his fellow-man as a tool merely, and injure him by that use; who would force another in any way to bend to his caprice; who would take advantage of his ignorance, his credulity, his superstition, or his poverty, to enrich and comfort himself; in a word, who would use his neighbor to his neighbor's hurt,—that man has the spirit of slave-holding, and were circumstances but different, he would chain his brethren with iron bonds. If you, for your own sake, would unjustly put any man in a position which degrades him in your eyes, in his own eyes, in the eyes of his fellow-men, you have the spirit of the slave-holder. There is much of this spirit with us still. . . . Doubtless we have still social institutions which eyes more Christian than ours shall one day look upon as evils, only less than that of slavery itself. But it is gradually that we gain light; he that converts it to life as fast as it comes, does well.

19 II. Let a word be said on the other kind of slavery; that which comes from a cause internal to ourselves. This is common at the North, and South, and East, and West. In this case the man is prevented from doing what is best for him, not by some other man who has bound him, but by some passion or prejudice, superstition or sin. Here the mischief is in his own heart. If you look around you, you find many that bear the mark of the beast; branded on the forehead and the right hand; branded as slaves. "He that committeth sin is the slave of sin." The avaricious man is a slave. He cannot think a thought but as his master bids. He cannot see a truth if a dollar intervene. He cannot relieve the poor, nor sympathize with the distressed, nor yield to the humane impulse of his natural heart. If he sees in the newspaper a sentence on the wastefulness or the idleness of the poor, he remembers it for ever; but a word in the Bible to encourage charity,—he never finds that.

20 The passionate man is a slave; he lies at the mercy of the accidents of a day. If his affairs go well he is calm and peaceful; but if some little mistake arise he is filled with confusion, and the demon that rules him draws the chain. This master has many a slave under his yoke. He is more cruel than any planter in Cuba or Trinidad. He not only separates friend from friend, parent from child, and husband from wife, but what is worse yet, prevents their loving one another while they are together. This makes man a tyrant, not a husband; woman a fiend, not an angel, as God made her to be. This renders marriage a necessary evil, and housekeeping a perpetual curse, for it takes the little trifles which happen everywhere, except between angels, and makes them very great matters; it converts mistakes into faults, accidents into vices, errors into crimes; and so rends asunder the peace of families, and in a single twelvemonth disturbs more marriages than all the slave-holders of Carolina in a century.

21 So the peevish man is a slave. His ill humour watches him like a demon. Ofttimes it casteth him into the fire, and often into the water. In the morning he

complains that his caprice is not complied with; in the evening that it is. He is
never peaceful except when angry; never quiet but in a storm. He is free to do
nothing good; so he acts badly, thinks badly, feels badly,—three attributes of a
devil. A yoke of iron and fetters of brass were grievous to bear, no doubt; the
whip of a task-master makes wounds in the flesh; but God save us from the
tyranny of the peevish, both what they inflict and what they suffer.

22 The intemperate man also is a slave; one most totally subjugated. His vice
exposes him to the contempt and insult of base men, as well as to the pity of the
good. Not only this, but his master strips him of his understanding; takes away
his common sense, conscience, his reason, religion,—qualities that make a man
differ from a beast; on his garments, his face, his wife and child, is written in
great staring letters, so that he may read that runs—This man also has sold his
birthright and becomes a slave. . . .

23 Bodily slavery is one of the greatest wrongs that man can inflict on man; an
evil not to be measured by the external and visible woe which it entails on the
victim, but by the deep internal ruin which it is its direct tendency to produce.
If I had the tongue of the Archangel I could not give utterance to the awfulness
of this evil. There is no danger that this be exaggerated,—no more than that the
sun in a picture be painted too bright. . . .

24 I know men say that you and I ought not to move in this matter; that we
have nothing to do with it. They urge in argument that the Constitution of the
United States is the supreme law of the land, and that sanctions slavery. But it
is the supreme law made by the voters, like the statutes denouncing capital
punishment. What voters have made can voters unmake. There is no supreme law
but that made by God; if our laws contradict that, the sooner they end or the
sooner they are broken, why, the better. It seems to be thought a very great thing
to run counter to a law of man, written on parchment; a very little thing to run
counter to the law of Almighty God, Judge of the quick and the dead. Has He
sanctioned slavery? "Oh yes," say some, and cite Old Testament and New
Testament in proof thereof. It has been said, "The devil can quote Scripture for
his purpose." We need not settle that question now, but it is certain that men can
quote it to support despotism when that is the order of the day,—or freedom
when that is the "law of the land;" certain that men defend drunkenness and war,
or sobriety and peace, out of its pages. A man finds what he looks for. . . .

25 Bodily slavery, though established by the powers that be, is completely in
the hands of the voters, for they are the powers that be, is no more sanctioned
by the supreme law of the land than stealing or murder. No enactment of man
can make that right which was wrong before. It can never be abstractly right in
any circumstances to do what is abstractly wrong.

26 But that other slavery, which comes from yourself, that is wholly within
your power. And which, think you, is the worse, to be unwillingly the slave of
a man and chained and whipped, or to be the voluntary slave of avarice, passion,
peevishness, intemperance! It is better that your body be forcibly constrained,
bought and sold, than that your soul, yourself, be held in thraldom. The spirit of

a slave may be pure as an angel's; sometimes as lofty and as blessed too. The comforts of religion, when the heart once welcomes them, are as beautiful in a slave's cabin as in a king's court. When death shakes off the slave's body, the chain falls with it, and the man, disenthralled at last, goes where the wicked cease from troubling, where the weary are at rest, where the slave is free from his master, yes, where faithful use of the smallest talent and humblest opportunity has its reward, and unmerited suffering finds its ample recompense. But the voluntary slavery under sin—it has no bright side. None in life; in death no more. You may flee from a taskmaster, not from yourself.

27 Body-slavery is so bad that the sun might be pardoned if it turned back, refusing to shine on such a sin; on a land contaminated with its stain. But soul-slavery, what shall we say of that? Our fathers bought political freedom at a great price; they sailed the sea in storms; they dwelt here aliens on a hostile soil, the world's outcasts; in cold and hunger, in toil and want they dwelt here; they fought desperate wars in freedom's name! Yet they bought it cheap. You and I were base men, if we would not give much more than they paid, sooner than lose the inheritance.

28 But freedom for the soul to act right, think right, feel right, you cannot inherit; that you must win for yourself. Yet it is offered you at no great price. You may take it who will. It is the birthright of you and me and each of us; if we keep its conditions it is ours. Yet it is only to be had by the religious man—the man true to the nature God gave him. Without His Spirit in your heart you have no freedom. Resist His law, revealed in nature, in the later scripture of the Bible, in your own soul; resist it by sin, you are a slave, you must be a slave. Obey that law, you are Christ's freeman; nature and God are on your side. How strange it would be that one man should be found on all the hills of New England, of soul so base, of spirit so dastardly, that of his own consent took on him the yoke of slavery; went into the service of sin; toiled with that leprous host, in hopeless unrecompensed misery, without God, without heaven, without hope. Strange, indeed, that in this little village there should be men who care not for the soul's freedom, but consent to live, no, to die daily, in the service of sin.

"THE MEXICAN WAR" (1849)

Parker's speech, "The Mexican War," was delivered at Faneuil Hall in Boston on February 4, 1849. Faneuil Hall is often referred to as the "Cradle of Liberty" because many of the events that culminated in the American Revolution happened there. Through the years it was the site where noted orators made important speeches. In the mid-nineteenth century, Daniel Webster, and noted abolitionists such as Wendell Phillips and Frederick Douglass applied their rhetoric at Faneuil Hall. Parker himself spoke there on several occasions.

Parker used this speech to attack the Mexican War as a "mean and infamous war," one waged "for the extension of slavery," so that there would be "yet more land to whip negroes in!" It was a short speech by Parker's standards, but it stands as one his most courageous. He challenged national and widely accepted policy, set by President Polk and the Congress, as illegal, a lie, unconstitutional, and a theft of Mexican land. Federal soldiers, armed with bayonets, surrounded the meeting. Polk had labeled sentiments, such as Parker expressed in this speech, to be treasonous in nature. Parker was sensitive to the charge. "Treason is it? . . . If my country is in the wrong, and I know it, and hold my peace, then I am guilty of treason, moral treason." There were those in the audience that day who vehemently denounced Parker as he spoke, calling out, "throw him over, kill him!" Parker took time in his speech to respond to the hecklers.

Parker often resorted to the use of parallelism throughout the speech—the repetition of a word or a group of words to begin sentences, phrases, and clauses. In the final paragraph, several sentences begin, "I call on . . ." and "because you . . ." Earlier in the speech Parker put together a series of phrases which began, "I blame . . ." and "in reference to. . ."

The speech is a primary example of how greatly moral principles motivated Parker, so that he would challenge any wrong or any power, regardless of the cost. Principles were everything, consequences of little importance. It is an exciting speech to read. One can only speculate on the experience of hearing it directly from Parker's lips in a tense and charged setting.

Mr. Chairman,—We have come hear to consult for the honor of our country. The honor and dignity of the United States are in danger. I love my country; I love her honor. It is dear to me almost as my own. I have seen stormy meetings at Faneuil Hall before now, and am not entirely disturbed by a popular tumult. But never before did I see a body of armed soldiers attempting to overawe the majesty of the people, when met to deliberate on the people's affairs. Yet the meetings of the people of Boston have been disturbed by soldiers before now, by British bayonets; but never since the Boston Massacre on the 5th of March, 1770! Our fathers hated a standing army. This is a new one, but behold the effect! Here are soldiers with bayonets to overawe the majesty of the people! They went to our meeting last Monday night, the hireling soldiers of President Polk, to overawe and disturb the meetings of honest men. Here they are now, and in arms!

We are in a war; the signs of war are seen here in Boston. Men, needed to hew wood and honestly serve society, are marching about your streets; they are learning to kill men, who never harmed us nor them; learning to kill their brothers. It is a mean and infamous war we are fighting. It is a great boy fighting a little one, and that little one feeble and sick. What makes it worse is, the little boy is in the right, and the big boy is in the wrong, and tells solemn lies to make his side seem right. He wants besides, to make the small boy pay the expenses of the quarrel.

The friends of the war say, "Mexico has invaded our territory!" When it is shown that it is we who have invaded hers, then it is said, "Ay, but she owes us money." Better say outright, "Mexico has land, and we want to steal it!"

This war is waged for a mean and infamous purpose, for the extension of slavery. It is not enough that there are fifteen slave States, and 8,000,000 men who have no legal rights—not so much as the horse and ox have in Boston; it is not enough that the slaveholdes annexed Texas, and made slavery perpetual therein, extending even north of Mason and Dixon's line, covering a territory forty-five times as large as the State of Massachusetts. Oh, no; we must have yet more land to whip negroes in!

The war had a mean and infamous beginning. It began illegally, unconstitutionally. The Whigs say, "The President made the war." Mr. Webster says so! It went on meanly and infamously. Your Congress lied about it. Do not lay the blame on the Democrats; the Whigs lied just as badly. Your Congress has seldom been so single-mouthed before. Why, only sixteen voted against the war, or the lie. I say this war is mean and infamous, all the more because waged by a people calling itself democratic and Christian. I know but one war so bad in modern times, between civilized nations, and that was the war for the partition of Poland. Even for that there was more excuse.

We have come to Faneuil Hall to talk about the war; to work against the war. It is rather late, but "better late than never." We have let two opportunities for work pass unemployed. One came while the annexation of Texas was pending. Then was the time to push and be active. Then was the time for Massachusetts and all the North, to protest as one man against the extension of slavery. Everybody knew all about the matter, the Democrats and the Whigs. But how few worked against that gross mischief? One man lifted up his warning voice; a man noble in his father—and there he stands in marble; noble in himself—and there he stands yet higher up;—and I hope time will show him yet, nobler in his son—and there he stands, not in marble, but in man! He talked against it, worked against it, fought against it. But Massachusetts did little. Her tonguey men said little; her handy men did little. Too little could not be done or said. True, we came here to Faneuil Hall and passed resolutions; good resolutions they were, too. Daniel Webster wrote them, it is said. They did the same in the State House; but nothing came of them. They say "Hell is paved with resolutions;" these were of that sort of resolutions, which resolve nothing, because they are of words, not works!

Well, we passed the resolutions; you know who opposed them; who hung back and did nothing—nothing good I mean; quite enough not good. Then we thought all the danger was over; that the resolutions settled the matter. But then was the time to confound at once the enemies of your country; to show an even front hostile to slavery.

But the chosen time passed over, and nothing was done. Do not lay the blame on the Democrats; a Whig Senate annexed Texas, and so annexed a war. We ought to have told our delegation in Congress, if Texas were annexed, to come home, and we would breathe upon it and sleep upon it, and then see what to do next. Had our resolutions, taken so warmly here in Faneuil Hall in 1845, been but as warmly worked out, we had now been as terrible to the slave power as the slave power, since extended, now is to us!

Why was it that we did nothing? That is a public secret. Perhaps I ought not to tell it to the people. (Cries of "Tell it.")

The annexation of Texas, a slave territory big as the kingdom of France, would not furl a sail on the ocean, would not stop a mill-wheel at Lowell! Men thought so.

That time passed by, and there came another. The Government had made war; the Congress voted the dollars, voted the men, voted a lie. Your representative men of Boston voted for all three—the lie, the dollars, and the men; all three, in obedience to the slave power! Let him excuse that to the conscience of his party; it is an easy matter. I do not believe he can excuse it to his own conscience. To the conscience of the world it admits of no excuse. Your President called for volunteers, 50,000 of them. Then came an opportunity such as offers not once in one hundred years, an opportunity to speak for freedom and the rights of mankind! Then was the time for Massachusetts to stand up in the spirit of '76, and say, "We won't send a man from Cape Ann to Williamstown—not one Yankee man, for this wicked war." Then was the time for your merchants to say, "Not a ship, not a dollar, for this wicked war;" for your manufacturers to say, "We will not make you a cannon, nor a sword, nor a kernel of powder, nor a soldier's shirt, for this wicked war." Then was the time for all good men to say, "This is a war for slavery, a mean and infamous war; an aristocratic war, a war against the best interests of mankind. If God please, we will die a thousand times, but never draw blade in this wicked war." (Cries of "Throw him over," etc.) Throw him over, what good would that do? What would you do next, after you have thrown him over? ("Drag you out of the hall!") What good would that do? It would not wipe off the infamy of this war! would not make it less wicked!

This is what a democratic nation, a Christian people ought to have said, ought to have done. But we did not say so; the Bay State did not say so, nor your Governor, nor your merchants, nor your manufacturers, nor your good men; the Governor accepted the President's decree, issued his proclamation calling for soldiers, recommended men to enlist, appealing to their "patriotism" and "humanity."

Governor Briggs is a good man; and so far I honor him. He is a temperance man, strong and consistent; I honor him for that. He is a friend of education; a friend of the people. I wish there were more such. Like many other New England men, he started from humble beginnings; but unlike many such successful men of New England, he is not ashamed of the lowest round he ever trod on. I honor him for all this. But that was a time which tried men's souls, and his soul could not stand the rack. I am sorry for him. He did as the President told him.

What was the reason for all this? Massachusetts did not like the war, even then; yet she gave her consent to it. Why so? There are two words which can drive the blood out of the cheeks of cowardly men in Massachusetts any time. They are "Federalism" and "Hartford Convention." The fear of those words palsied the conscience of Massachusetts, and so her Governor did as he was told.

I feel no fear of either. The Federalists did not see all things; who ever did? They had not the ideas which were destined to rule this nation; they looked back when the age looked forward. But to their own ideas they were true; and if ever a nobler body of men held state in any nation, I have yet to learn when or where. If we had the shadow of Caleb Strong in the Governor's chair, not a volunteer for this war had gone out of Massachusetts.

I have not told quite all the reasons why Massachusetts did nothing. Men knew the war would cost money; that the dollars would in the end be raised, not by a direct tax, of which the poor man paid according to his little, and the rich man in proportion to his much; but by a tariff which presses light on property, and hard on the person—by a tax on the backs and mouths of the people. Some of the Whigs were glad last spring when the war came, for they hoped thereby to save the child of their old age, the tariff of '42. There are always some rich men, who say, "No matter how much the nation suffers, if we fill our hungry purses thereby." Well, they lost their virtue, lost their tariff, and gained just nothing, what they deserved to gain.

Now a third opportunity has come;—no, it has not come; we have brought it. The President wants a war tax on tea and coffee. Is that democratic, to tax every man's breakfast and supper, for the sake of getting more territory to whip negroes in? (Numerous cries of "Yes.") Then what do you think despotism would be? He asks a loan of $8,000,000 to spend privately for this war. In eight months past, he has asked, I am told, for $74,000,000. Seventy-four million of dollars to conquer slave territory! Is that democratic too? He wants to increase the standing army, to have ten regiments more! A pretty business that. Ten regiments to gag the people in Faneuil Hall, do you think that is democratic? Some men have just asked Massachusetts for $20,000 for the volunteers! It is time for the people to rebuke all this wickedness.

I think there is a good deal to excuse the volunteers. I blame then for some of them know what they are about. Yet, I pity them more, for most of them, I am told, are low, ignorant men, some of them drunken and brutal. From the uproar they make here to-night, arms in their hands, I think what was told me is true! I say, I pity them. They are my brothers, not the less brothers because low and misguided. If they are so needy that they are forced to enlist by poverty, surely I pity them. If they are of good families, and know better, I pity them still more! I blame most the men that have duped the rank and file! I blame the captains and colonels, who will have least of the hardships, most of the pay, and all of the "glory." I blame the men that made the war; the men that make money out of it. I blame the great party men of the land. Did not Mr. Clay say he hoped he could slay a Mexican! (Cries, "No, he didn't.") Yes, he did; said it on Forefather's day! Did not Mr. Webster, in the streets of Philadelphia, bid the volunteers, misguided young men, go and uphold the stars of their country! (Voices, "He did right!") No; he should have said the stripes of his country, for every volunteer to this wicked war is a stripe on the nation's back! Did not he declare this war unconstitutional, and threaten to impeach the President who made it, and then go and invest a son in it? Has it not been said here, "Our country, howsoever bounded," bounded by robbery or bounded by right lines! Has it not been said, all round, "Our country, right or wrong!"

I say, I blame not so much the volunteers as the famous men who deceived the nation! (Cries of "Throw him over; kill him, kill him!" and a flourish of bayonets.) Throw him over! you will not throw him over. Kill him! I shall walk unarmed and unattended and not a man of you will hurt one hair of my head.

I say again, it is time for the people to take up this matter. Your Congress will do nothing till you tell them what and how. Your 29th Congress can do little good. Its sands are nearly run, God be thanked! It is the most infamous Congress we ever had. We began with the Congress that declared Independence, and swore by the eternal justice of God. We have come down to the 29th Congress, which declared war existed by the act of Mexico—declared a lie; the Congress that swore by the Baltimore Convention! We began with George Washington, and have got down to James K. Polk.

It is time for the people of Massachusetts to instruct their servants in Congress to oppose this war; to refuse all supplies for it; to ask for the recall of the army into our own land. It is time for us to tell them that not an inch of slave territory shall ever be added to the realm. Let us remonstrate; let us petition; let us command. If any class of men have hitherto been remiss, let them come forward now and give us their names—the merchants, the manufacturers, the Whigs and the Democrats. If men love their country better than their party or their purse, now let them show it.

Let us ask the General Court of Massachusetts to cancel every commission which the Governor has given to the officers of the volunteers. Let us ask them to disband the companies not yet mustered into actual service; and then, if you like that, ask them to call a convention of the people of Massachusetts, to see what we shall do in reference to the war; in reference to the annexation of more territory; in reference to the violation of the Constitution. (Loud groans from crowds of rude fellows in several parts of the hall.) That was a Tory groan; they never dared groan so in Faneuil Hall before; not even the British Tories, when they had no bayonets to back hem up! I say, let us ask for these things!

Your President tells us it is treason to talk so! Treason is it? treason to discuss a war which the Government made, and which the people are made to pay for? If it be treason to speak against the war, what was it to make the war, to ask for 50,000 men and $74,000,000 for the war? Why, if the people cannot discuss the war they have got to fight and to pay for, who under heaven can? Whose business is it, if it is not yours and mine? If my country is in the wrong, and I know it, and hold my peace, then I am guilty of treason, moral treason. Why, a wrong—it is only the threshold of ruin. I would not have my country take the next step. Treason is it, to show that this war is wrong and wicked? Why, what if George III, any time from '75 to '85, had gone down to Parliament and told them it was treason to discuss the war then waging against these colonies! What do think the Commons would have said? What would the Lords say? Why, that king, foolish as he was, would have been lucky, if he had not learned there was a joint in his neck, and, stiff as he bore him, that the people knew how to find it.

I do not believe in killing kings, or any other men; but I do say, in a time when the nation was not in danger, that no British king, for two hundred years past, would have dared call it treason to discuss the war—its cause, its progress, or it termination!

Now is the time to act! Twice we have let the occasion slip; beware of the third time! Let it be infamous for a New England man to enlist; for a New England merchant to loan his dollars, or to let his ships in aid of this wicked war; let it be infamous for a manufacturer to make a cannon, a sword, or a kernel of powder to kill our brothers with, while we all know that they are in the right, and we in the wrong.

I know my voice is a feeble one in Massachusetts. I have no mountainous position from whence to look down and overawe the multitude; I have no background of political reputation to echo my words. I am but a plain, humble man; but I have a background of truth to sustain me, and the justice of heaven arches over my head! For your sakes, I wish I had that oceanic eloquence whose tidal flow should bear on its bosom the drift-wood which politicians have piled together, and sap and sweep away the sand-hillocks of soldiery blown together by the idle wind; that oceanic eloquence which sweeps all before it, and leaves the shore hard, smooth, and clean! But feeble as I am, let me beg of you, fellow-citizens of Boston, men and brothers, to come forward and protest against this wicked war, and the end for which it is waged. I call on the Whigs, who love their country better than they love the tariff of '42; I call on the Democrats, who think justice is greater than the Baltimore convention,—I call on the Whigs and Democrats to come forward and join with me in opposing this wicked war! I call on the men of Boston, on the men of the old Bay State, to act worthy of their fathers, worthy of their country, worthy of themselves! Men and brothers, I call on you all to protest against this most infamous war, in the name of the State, in the name of the country, in the name of man—yes, in the name of God; leave not your children saddled with a war debt, to cripple the nation's commerce for years to come. Leave not your land cursed with slavery, extended and extending, palsying the nation's arm and corrupting the nation's heart. Leave not your memory infamous among the nations, because you feared men, feared the Government; because you loved money got by crime, land plundered in war, loved land unjustly bounded; because you debased your country by defending the wrong she dared to do; because you loved slavery, loved war, but loved not the eternal justice of all-judging God. If my counsel is weak and poor, follow one stronger and more manly. I am speaking to men; think of these things and then act like men!

"THE REVIVAL OF RELIGION WHICH WE NEED" (1858)

This sermon was delivered before Parker's congregation at the Music Hall on Sunday, April 11, 1858. It was a time of evangelical revivalism in the United States. Parker's sermon was critical of much of the contemporary religious fervor, because it was challenging people to devote themselves to correct doctrine rather than to true piety and morality. True religion, according to Parker, filled people with unspeakable joy. "In all the world . . . there is nothing so joyous as real natural religion. It is the contromost of all delights." True religion also addressed the major evils of society, which Parker listed as war, character of government, slavery, the antagonist character of civilization, and the condition of women. Most ministers, Parker accused, failed to address these issues, instead "they aim chiefly to remove unbelief in ecclesiastical doctrines, to admit them to the church, to save their souls from the wrath of God by belief in the magic of atonement." Notice the number of times in the sermon when Parker refers to God as "Father and Mother." The finest contemporary example of true religion, Parker affirmed, was Emerson. "No living man has done so much as Emerson to waken this Religion in the great Saxon heart of Americans and Britons. It is not doctrine he teaches—his own creed is not well defined . . . but his words and his life charm earnest men with such natural religion as makes them, of their own accord, to trust the Great Soul of all, and refine themselves into noble, normal, individual life."

"Be ye perfect, even as your Father which is in heaven is heaven is perfect."
MATT. v.48.

Last Sunday I said something of a False and True Revival of Religion. Today I continue the same theme, asking your attention to some thoughts on the Revival of Religion which we need, and the Way to bring it to pass.

In the World of Man there is nothing so joyous as real natural religion. Other high joys are branches, this the root they run back to, spring out of, and grow up from. I feel gratitude to many a man and woman who has helped me in my life, but to none such thankfulness as I owe my mother, my father, my sister, for the pains they took to develop this innermost of all the facts of Consciousness. I cannot remember the earliest twilight of religion when first I felt the "dayspring from on high," not even the rising of that sun which sheds such light to all my being. I trust it will not reach its noon until I have seen some four or five score years, but will rise higher, shining with more perpendicular glory until I end my mortal life. For religion grows not old. Like God, it flourishes in perpetual youth.

I too have experienced the higher joys of life; thereof not many men know better what is great in bulk; few more what is nice and exquisite in kind. Have science, letters, success, a joy to give? I know it reasonably well. Is there joy in contending with difficulties? I have had my part. Are there pleasures of affection? I have tasted from that golden cup, and by those I love can drink vicariously at many a spring my lips never directly touch. But dear and blessed as are all these things, I count them cheap compared with my delight in God. These I could renounce and still be blessed, at least resigned, but not to know the Father and Mother of the world, to feel shut out from that causal and providential Love, which creates all from itself, I should go mad and die at once, or live a maimed, brutal life, and perish like a fool. But of this cheap joy, I cannot speak save in the most general terms. 'Tis profane to talk of such things even to most intimate friends. The handsome shapes of our innermost life are chastely veiled from all the world; there I am my own high priest, and into that Holy of Holies none but myself and Thou, O God! can ever come.

Does not mankind also rate the religious consciousness thus high? Whom does it honor most? Always its heroes of the soul. Men with genius for religion. Such men as Moses, Buddha, Jesus, Mohammed, they are above all human names. None else have such millions bowing thereto; none others are worshipped so as Gods. How thankful we are to whoever brings religious truths! Mankind is loyal, and when it sees its King, takes him to its heart, and honors Him forever. Thankful to those who helped us, with what sympathy do we look on persons trying to attain religious excellence! No romance is so attractive to us all as the story of a man longing after God and seeking rest for the soul. How do you and I, seeking such, wish to go to this child crying in the darkness, wet and numb with cold, and like a great Saint Christopher to take him on our shoulders and thus ferry him across the stream, warming his limbs while we bear him wrapped in our mantle, and then you put a candle in his lantern and bread in his pouch and bid him "God speed you my brother! You will find day bye and bye!"

When a great truth stirs the feelings infinite within us, how do we love to show the cause thereof to other men, and set slips from the tree of life in their gardens to make a new Paradise! Worldly ambition is singular—for itself alone; the passion of love is dual—for him and her; but the affection of religion is universal—plural, embracing God and all his world within rejoicing arms. Nothing is so socializing as piety; my Father and my Mother they are also yours.

No man is complete without the culture of the religious element; no high faculty perfect without help from that. I see great naturalists without it, great politicians, great artists; not great men. Nay, then special science, politics, art, is less philosophic, statesmanlike, aesthetic, for lack of this wholeness and thorough health within the man's interior. The notes of music, ground out on a hand organ in the street, tell me if their composer had ever listened to the quiring of these birds of Paradise.

There is a story—perhaps some of you never heard it—that out of Parian stone a great Christian artist in the dark ages, once carved a statue of the Virgin Mary—the Church's ideal woman. It was transcendent of mortality, angels, disdainful of earth, fit only for the devotional delights of heaven, not womanly duty on earth, and sympathy of suffering and sinful man. He wrought so fair that Phidias and Praxiteles and many a Heathen more who knew the wondrous art to transfigure marble into life, through their open graves came back from heaven to look thereon; and filled with joy at this new type of womanhood, so different

from the Aphrodites and Athenas, so free alike from sensual taint and oligarchic
pride of intellect and power, with their cold, dumb, visionary mouths, they kissed
the plastic hand which wrought the wondrous work. But Mary herself—no
queenly virgin transcending earth, but peasant Joseph's honest wife and natural
mother of his boy—came also back from her heavenly transformation. Well
pleased she looked thereon, but was not quite content, loving the natural woman
of humanity, a carpenter's wife and mother to boys and girls in Nazareth, more
than she loved non-human, transcendental virgin of the Church's creed, fit only
for heavenly joy; and so she put a live branch of Hebrew lilies, sweet as these
New England violets, wet with dew, into the statue's folded hand. Fair were they
as the marble, but living flowers, which grew out of the hard black ground and
bore their seed within them, to fill the earth with future loveliness. And this
piece of actual nature, surpassing the sculptor's art, so criticized his dreamy
stone, that when he woke and saw it there, he felt rebuked and took the heavenly
hint, and ever after fashioned his Madonnas complete woman, of nobler and
more actual shape—not monsters, virgins of the sky, but women, sisters, wives,
mothers, for the world of time, the mortal, earthly, beauty kept and made more
fair and human by its wholeness and its complete and perfect trust in the dear
God who fashioned woman's body and inspired her soul. And as the sign that
such dear divinity yet touched the common ground, he put the emblematic lilies
in the statue's folded hand.

So when I see a man, else grand and beautified, with transcendent mind and
conscience and affection too, but lacking this ultimate finish of religion, I long
to plant therein the soul of piety which shall complete the whole and so make
perfect every part—mastering the world of time, but not disclaiming it.

I have heard of many conversions—here is the story of a real one. A man
was a drunkard, noisy, violent; he beat his wife and children, nay, his mother.
Crossing yonder bridge one dark night, all at once his own conscience spoke in
him—"Stop there, Richard! Drink no more!" Not disobedient unto the heavenly
vision, he stopped, and swore to drink no more. He became a new man. There
was a revival of religion in him,—at least a part of it; ever after he had
Temperance, the piety of the flesh. Some of you understand that conversion. To
speak as ministers—Jacob wrestles with the devil all night, flings him, and goes
off conqueror, the devil down, and the man up for all time. Honor to conversions
of this stamp!

What a joy it would be if there could come to pass a real Revival of
Religion, of Piety and Morality, in the churches of America—I mean among the
thirty thousand Protestant ministers and the thirty hundred thousand Protestant
church members;—a Revival of Religion which should be qualitatively nice and
quantitatively large,—a great, new growth of the soul; such a healthy bloom of
piety as would make a White-Sunday all over the land, prophetic of whole
Messianic harvests of Piety and Morality, which were to come! Why, if such a
thing were to take place, and I were Governor of Massachusetts or President of
the United States, though it were seed-time or harvest-time, war-time even, I

would issue my proclamation for a Day of Thanksgiving and Praise to the dear God who had given such gifts unto men. I would ask the people to come together in their meeting-houses, look each other in the face, take each other by the hand, embrace, and sing their psalms of praise to the infinite Father and Mother, whose kingdom had come on earth, and was shining as the sun from east to west. I would call on great orators for choicest speech; on the poets, "blest with the vision and the faculty divine" and furnished with "the accomplishment of verse," to sing the High Song and Canticles of joy,—the great Psalms of glorifying praise to Him who is Power, Wisdom, Justice, Love. Nay, I would send my Ambassadors to the nations of the earth, saying, "Come and rejoice with me, for this my son was dead and is alive again, he was lost and is found." Nay, if such a movement went on in England, France, Italy, Spain, Turkey, Egypt, Arabia, Palestine, I would ask you to spare me for awhile, and would strike work to-morrow, that I might go and sacrament my eyes with the sight of the happy people that is in such a case. I would learn how that great salvation was brought about, and fetch home in my garments the Promethean seed of that fire, to kindle a flame all over the land.

Only think of it! a Revival of piety, a new power of love to God, and love for all his laws, writ in the flesh and spirit, mind and conscience, heart and soul, and a consequent love of morality—the will and conscience going side by side, like Caleb and Joshua, bringing home such clusters from the promised land; and increase of intellect, power of use, power of beauty, power of truth; a great growth of economy, industry, riches; the heaven of chaste love.—Passion and Affection going hand in hand, taking sweet counsel together, and walking to the house of God in company; the growth of justice, humanity, charity. Only think of it! Forts turned into pleasure grounds; all training fields, "converted" into public gardens; ships of war the penny-posters of the deep; arsenals changed into museums; jails become hospitals; not a gallows in America; slavery all ended; black slavery, white slavery; no murder; no theft; prostitution gone; no bestial lust anywhere, but human love forever; poverty ended; drunkenness all banished; no staggering in the street; not an Irishman drunk,—not even a member of Congress; no kidnapper between the seas; no liar in the chair of Governor or broker; rulers that love the people, enacting justice; ministers teaching them the truths of nature and of human consciousness—proclaiming the real live God, who inspires men to-day, as He dresses these roses in their sweet cloth of gold. Think of a Revival of Religion such as that which was bringing that about, which would do it in a hundred years or a thousand! Why, what were all the previous great triumphs of mankind to that? What were the conquests of fire, iron, the invention of ships, letters, powder, the compass, the printing press, the steam engine, telegraph, ether? What was the discovery of America, the English Revolution, the American, the French? Nay, what were these six great historic forms of religion—Brahminic, Hebraistic, Classic, Buddhistic. Christian, Mohammedan—they would be what February and March are to May, July, September and October; what a few weeks of thaw are to a whole summer of flowers and an autumn full of fruit. Why, the very sympathizing sun might pause in his course and gladden his eyes, and the stars of heaven, which have seen their image reflected back in a looking-glass of human blood, might stop and join in that primal mythic psalm, "Glory to God in the highest, on earth peace, to all good willing men."

How much we need a real Revival of Religion! Not a renewal of Ecclesiastic Theology, but a Revival of Piety and Morality in men's hearts.

The people feel this need; hence we turn off to look at all new things in religion. We are tired of that old stack of hard, dry, meadow hay, where the Christian herd has so long sought fodder, and been filled with the east wind. We long for the green pastures and sweet grass along the streams which run among the hills; hence we wish to leap over or crawl under or crowd through the bars of this old winter cow-yard of the church, and at least get out of that unwholesome pen and go somewhere, with God to guide us, though we know not whither.

See the growth of Mormonism. Even that has something that mankind needs; else men, and especially women, would not cross the sea three thousand miles wide, and then travel three thousand more by river or by land for its sake. The success of Mormonism is a terrible protest against the enforced celibacy of millions of marriageable women, and the worse than celibacy of so many who are called married, but are not. Fifteen years ago, "Spiritualism" was two women making mysterious noises in Rochester, N. Y. Now it is I know not how many millions of persons, some of them thoughtful, many hungering after God. "Spiritualism" had something to offer which the churches could not give. Nothing comes of nothing, every something has a cause. This very Revival, foolish as is the conduct of it, selfish as are the managers who pull the strings,—with the people it indicates a profound discontent in the dull death of our churches. God created man a living soul, and he continues such only by feeding on every word which freshly proceedeth out of the mouth of God. The old bibles did for those who wrote them; the old creeds for such as believed. We want the help of the old bibles, the inspiration of the new bibles, ever proceeding from God, who freshly fills the old stars in heaven, and new flowers every spring on earth.

I say the people feel the need; but the need itself is greater and deeper than the popular consciousness thereof. We do not know how sick we are. Look at the chaotic state of things in America, which is like the rest of Christendom. First, there is war. Fenced with a two-fold oceanic ditch, from two to seven thousand miles wide, we yet spend more than thirty millions of dollars every year to hire fighting men, in a time of profound peace; and not one of them fixes bayonets to do mankind good.

Next consider the character of the Federal Government—it is the last place to which you would look for common honesty, for justice to our nation; just now it is a vulture which eats the nation's vitals out; only the strong giant grows faster than this administration can tear off and swallow down. Men tell us human life is more safe in Constantinople, in Damascus, in Samareand, in Timbuctoo, than it is in Washington. We are told that we have three murders a fortnight in the Capital of the United States, all the session through. The Government is so busy filibustering against Cuba, Mexico, Central America, planting slavery in Kansas, that it cannot protect the lives of its own Congressman in its own Capital.

Next look at slavery. Every seventh man is property—a negro slave; and our Supreme Court says colored people have no rights which we are bound to respect. The Government seeks to spread this blot across the continent, from east to west, from south to north—asks five thousand new soldiers to do it with. A new State knocks at the door, seeking to join the sisterhood of Freedom; the Government says, "You shall not come in free; with bondsmen you may enter."

Fourth: Look at the antagonistic character of our civilization. So much poverty in the midst of so much riches—so many idlers in so much industry. How many children in prudent, wealthy, charitable Boston, cannot go to school in winter from lack of clothes! See what fortunes are dishonestly made, by men who are only the filibusters of commerce, robbers in a peaceful way. Our industry even now is a war of business—it is competition, not co-operation. How much power is lost in the friction of our social machinery. There are savages in our civilization. In the south, many of them are slaves—in the north, they are free, but still savages. A black sea of crime lashes the white houses of wealth and comfort, where science, literature, virtue and piety together dwell.

Fifth: Look at the condition of women. There is no conscious antagonism between men and women; each doubtless unconsciously aims to be more than fair to the other; but nowhere has woman her natural right. In the market, the state, the church, she is not counted the equal of man. Hence come monstrous evils—prostitution, dependence, lack of individual character, enforced celibacy, not more grateful to maid than to man, meant for neither him nor her; and hence come those marriages which are worse than celibacy itself.

These are the five great evils of mankind to-day, whence many lesser ones proceed—drunkenness, crime in its thousand forms. I do not speak to scold mankind, still less to scold America. In all respects save one, we have the best institutions in the world; and certainly, the human race had never so glorious a welfare as to-day. These evils, they were never before so small. History, is not a retreat back-wards, it is progress forth, upwards, on. These things are not a finality; they are to man's attainable condition what stumbling is to walking, stammering to speech, the boy's clumsy, mistaken scrawl to the clear current writing of the man. We are to outlearn these five evils—war, wicked government, slavery, selfish antagonism in society, the degradation of women. We shall outgrow these things. God has given us the fittest of all possible means for attaining the end. One of man's mightiest helpers is this Religious Faculty in us; this, nothing else, can give us strength to do that work.

The business of the farmer is to organize the vegetative force of the ground, and raise thence the substances which shall feed and clothe mankind. The mechanic is to organize the forces of metals, wood, fire, earth, water, lightning, air, and thereby shape the material things necessary to human needs—to feed, clothe, house, and heal mankind; corn he must turn into bread, cotton and wool to cloth, the clay, the forest, the rock, to houses; poison to medicine. The philosopher is to translate the facts of nature, from matter into mind, making them into thoughts, ideas of consciousness, then to show us how to use the powers of nature, for the farmer's and mechanic's work. The statesman is to organize the nation's power, its matter and its mind, its bodily force, its wealth, intelligence, justice, love, charity, religion, so that men shall live in peace together at home, with peace abroad, having security for the person, the substance for mankind; so that each shall help all, and all enjoy the special genius God gives to each.

It is the business of the minister to waken, quicken, strengthen, and guide the religious faculty, and to gain for us a great general power to help the individual man, in his development of body and of spirit. But man is social. The individual alone is a wild man; it is only in society that noble individualism is instantially possible. While these five evils just named continue, individual man will be as now. It is in the great social mill that men are made what they are. Here and there may be one so born, that society cannot shape, bleach, or dye the man. He takes up form or color, save from his mother's bosom, he had an impenetrable genius from his birth,—plastic to mould others, not pliant to be shaped or dyed. But in ninety-nine hundredths of our characters, most men are what society makes them. Compare Old England and New England, the children of Cove Place with the children of Beacon Street, to see the truth of this, the power of circumstances over the soul.

It is the minister's business not only to waken, and strengthen, and quicken the religious power, and bend it to this end, but also to diffuse the ideas which shall mould society, so that it can rear noble men, with all their natural powers developed well.

The minister is the teacher of the church, not a master; a servant, to teach. A normal church is a body of men, assembling to promote Religion, Piety and Morality. Its business is, first, protective at home—to promote piety and morality in its own members; and second, it is diffusive abroad—to promote piety and morality in all the world according to its strength: for duty is proportionate to power to do; and when the power is little, so is the duty, where much, there great. So a church must protest against all wrong which it knows to be wrong; promote all right which it knows to be right. It is a church for that very purpose, and nothing less. The minister is to help do that work; to lead in it. He must be in advance of mankind in what pertains to religion—to all religion, individual, social. Else he cannot teach, he is no minister to work and serve, only an idler to be worked for and ministered unto.

No doubt there must be primary churches, to teach the A, B, C, of religion, and ministers fit for that work of nursing babies; and also academic and collegiate churches, and ministers for that grand function. Let neither despise the other. So, then, the function of a real church of religion will be partly creative, to show us the right and guide us thither, at least thither-ward.

We have thirty thousand Protestant ministers in the United States, supported at the public charge, and to do this very work, for so the people mean. They are not rich; are not rich men's sons. As a class, they have an education which is costly, even when it is not precious; which if often paid for directly by the people's work. All education is thus paid for indirectly, for in that money all human accounts are at last settled, in the great clearing house of mankind. Work is the only coin which is current the world over. Therein do you pay for the murders which are committed at Washington, and for the Angels of Mercy, who in Boston carry your beneficence from house to house, and take unlawful babies; newly born, and set them in religious homes, to grow up to nobleness. In that coin we pay for all things,—the minister's education amongst others. The ministers come mainly from that class of people who are most affected by religious emotions and ideas, where human sympathies are the strongest. They seldom are borne by the miserably poor, or the ruinously rich. They have two great advantages: Birth in the middle class, where they touch the ground and touch the sky; and superior culture above that class. Add to this, moreover, they commonly enter the ministry with good motives, more self-denial than self-indulgence; they are usually free from gross vices, the crimes of passion; and are the most charitable of alms giving men; they have the best opportunities to teach the churches; and to help promote the critical and creative function which belongs thereto.

But now, alas! taken as a class, they do no such thing,—they attempt none such. They do not count it their business to remove any one of those five great social evils, and so enable society to raise up noble and individual men. Nay, they seldom take much pains to remove the lesser evils which have leaked out from those five great tubs of malarious poison. Let the prayers of the Protestant churches be answered to-night; let all the white men and women of the United States be converted to the Ecclesiastical Theology which is taught in Orthodox meeting houses; let the conversion take in all the babies who know their right hand from their left—suppose there are fifteen millions who are "brought under," and "bowed down," as they probably call it, and made to believe in the creeds of the Revival ministers; let all these be added to the Church next Sunday and take their communion of baker's bread and grocer's wine,—it would not abate one of those five great evils—War, Political Corruption, Slavery, Selfish Antagonism in Society, nor the Degradation of Women! Such a conversion is not a step towards removing any one of these evils—nay, it is a step away from that work. Such a conversion would entail inferiority on women; retard the progress of civilization, the moralization of mankind; add to the fetters of the slave; strengthen the tyrant's hand, increase the chances of prospective war, and add to its horrors when it broke out. For it would bless all these iniquities in the name of God, and justify them out of the Old Testament and the New—it is quite easy to do so. Nay, suppose you should convert the three millions of African slaves over ten years old, not one of them would dare thereafter to run away from his master, or strike that master down. Such conversions would unman the negro slave!

Why is all this? Two months ago, I spoke of the False Methods of Theology. The Christian Church followed that method, and while teaching many truths and doing very great service to mankind—which I should be the last to deny—it made three monstrous errors. Here they are.

First, it has a false conception of God;—its God is a devil, who means damnation.

Second, it has a false conception of man;—its man is a worm, who is religiously good for nothing; the "natural man" fit only for damnation.

Third, it has a false conception of Religion;—its Religion is to save men from hell, and is fit only for that. But it does not do even that for more than one out of a thousand; for the other nine hundred and ninety-nine, it is absolutely good for nothing on earth or beneath it; and the one saved is not borne to heaven on mighty wings of piety and morality, fanning the thin cold air of the world, but by the magic-miracle of the atonement, which turns off God's wrath, and carries man into eternal joy which he has done nothing to merit and to earn.

These Ideas are the minister's tools to work with. I am not scolding him, only stating facts. Poor man! he is far more to be pitied than blamed. He sees a vast amount of evil in the world, and thinks it all a finality; it is God's will, and his decree that it shall last forever. The evil cannot be removed here and now,—it is in the nature of things; and even in the next life, it will never be diminished to all eternity. Man cannot remove it; God will not; for He loves none but Church members, who believe the Church Theology; He will ruin all else;—and damned for once is damned for evermore.

Hence ministers in churches do not make it a principal thing to try and remove these evils, to develop man's nature, to set the religious faculty, that greatest River of God, to turn the morals of society. They aim chiefly to remove unbelief in ecclesiastical doctrines, to admit men to the church, to save their souls from the wrath of God by belief in the magic of atonement. "No man," say they, "goes into heaven for his religion, for any merit of his own; with a whole life of piety and morality, ended in the cruelest martyrdom, he cannot buy a ticket of entrance," while a moment's belief in the ecclesiastic theology, and joining of a church, will admit a pirate, a kidnapper, a deceitful politician who curses a nation, or a hypocritical priest—it will admit them all to heaven—each man as a "dead-head."

Do you doubt that the churches of America count not merely religious character and life, but only theological belief as the one thing needful?—then look at these two facts.

First, the Protestant Churches of America have one great corporation—the Tract Society—wherein many sects work together. The aim is theological—to enforce ecclesiastic doctrines; it is not religious—to promote love to God, and the keeping of his natural laws writ in the very constitution of man. So the Tract

Society protests against none of the great evils I have named. It attacks no popular wickedness; it would save men from the fancied wrath of God by faith in Christ; not by virtue and wisdom save them from actual ignorance, superstition, covetousness, drunkenness, dishonesty. It would save men *in* their sins hereafter, not *from* their sins to-day and here. It has little to say against war, political oppression, slavery, the antagonism of society, the degradation of woman. Even the bible society, in which all sects unite, dares not give the New Testament to a single slave, though the American anti-slavery Society offer them Five Thousand Dollars if they will spend it thus. Spite of its profession, spite of its good intention, the church is baptized worldliness, professing the ecclesiastical theology as magical means of salvation from the future consequences of a life of wickedness below!

That is the first thing. Next, many Christian ministers think they can tease God to do what they want done; that they can get him to convert men, and if the prayers of the churches center on one man, he presently "caves in." Now, at a Revival meeting, who is prayed for, prayed at, prayed against? The Ecclesiastical archers do not draw their bow at a venture; it is with good aim. What Saint Sebastian is there who is stuck full of the arrows of Calvinistic imprecation? Is it the sly, corrupt politician? the "democrat" who hates democracy, but under its covert seeks to ruin the people? No; he is orthodox in profession, though atheistic in his public practice and private creed. Is it the able lawyer, who prostitutes his grand talents to bring the most miserable culprit safe from the justice of the law? No; Sunday after Sunday he sits in an orthodox meeting-house, and requires no conversion. Is it the capitalist who rents his shops for drunkaries and gambling dens, his houses, for brothels? No; he is sound in the faith. Is it the merchant who trades in Coolies? No; he is a church member, painted with the proper stripe. Is it the Doctor of Divinity who defends Slavery as a Divine institution? Not at all; he believes in the damnation of Unitarians, Universalists and babies not wet with baptism; he needs no repentance. Is it the trader, whose word is good for nothing, who will always take you in? No; he is out in the street pimping for the prayer-meetings of his sect. Is it the man who sends rum and gunpowder to the negroes of Africa, and fills his ship with slaves for Cuba, half of them cast shrieking to the hungry waves before it touches land? Oh no; he contributes to the Tract Society. Do men pray for the President of the United States, that in his grand position, with his magnificent opportunities, he may secure to all men the "unalienable right to life, liberty, and the pursuit of happiness"?—may take the Golden Rule of this blessed New Testament and make that a meet-wand for the American Government? They ask no such thing. Do they pray that our Supreme Court may "do justly, and love mercy, and walk humbly with its God?" They pray for no such men; and those they do pray for, they ask only that they may believe the creed, and "come to Christ." To Jesus of Nazareth! It does not mean to come to him who said religion was love to God and love to man! It means only, come to the Catechism and the meeting house!

I do not know how many men, and women too, have labored with me to convert me. Not one ever asked me to increase in Religion, in either part of it—in Piety or Morality; to be more temperate, industrious, truth-telling—quite the opposite of that; more generous, just, charitable, philanthropic, forgiving to my enemies. Not one ever asked me to be a better minister, scholar, neighbor, friend, cousin, uncle, brother, husband. None ever prayed me to love God better, or to keep his commandments more, only to "come to Christ;" and their Christ, it was the Catechism, which tormented me in my infancy, which I sobbed over many a night and wept myself to sleep, and at last made away with the abominable thing, trod it under my feet forever, before I had seen my seventh birth-day. I do not know how many letter-writers, clergymen, laymen, and lay women visitors, have threatened me with eternal damnation. This one is sure I am to have it at last; these others declare it is coming "summarily." No one ever charged me with any vice, with any lack of virtue or manly excellence; only with disbelief in the Catechism. That is the second thing.

These two things show that the church wants belief in the theology of unreason, not a life of natural piety and morality; and because the ministers work for this, and with such tools to this end, is it that so many of them pass their lives

"In dropping buckets into empty wells,
And growing old in drawing nothing up."

These things being so, Ecclesiastical Revivals do no considerable good. They make superstitious church members, no religious men and women. "They heal the hurt of the daughters of my people slightly"—I mean, they do not heal it at all.

"They skin and film the ulcerous place
Whilst rank corruption, mining all within,
Infects unseen."

What is the great obstacle to the liberation of France, Spain, Italy? It is the Roman church; and if every Frenchman was a member of the Roman church, and believed its creed, France might give up the ghost to-morrow—it would never be free.

What is the great obstacle to the improvement of Catholics in America? It is the Catholic church; and just in proportion as an Irishman is wedded to that church, just so do I despair of him. In a less degree, our Protestant Theology is working a similar harm for us.

I believe in a Revival of Religion. There have been several great movements thereof. Not to go out of the Hebrew and Christian church, there are several well known to all of you. That of Moses, Jesus, Luther, the Puritans, the Quakers, the Baptists, the Methodists, Unitarians, Universalists, and the Spiritualists. How were they brought about? In each case, there was a new Theologic idea, by a man of genius, or a new application of an old one by a man of talent. Moses taught the people—"There is one God for the Hebrews, to be served by ritual sacrifices in one place." Jesus declared—"There is one God for all mankind, to be served by brotherly love. The walls of Nationality are broke down." Luther taught,—"The infallible Bible is superior to a deceitful Pope. There is freedom of conscience for all men; they are justified by faith in Christ, not by the ritual of Roman priests. Each people must manage its own church affairs." The Puritans declared—"Each church must manage its own affairs, the Bible its only law." The Baptists declared—"Grown men must be baptized all over. No man goes into heaven dry-shod; the priest must wet him from heel to crown. He that believeth and is *immersed,* shall be saved." The Quaker said—"The Holy Ghost *in* the soul is more than the letter of Scripture *out* of it. Man is free. Not bound by his father's ordinances. Woman is man's equal. The prayer that God hears is in the heart; He needs no words to understand it." The Methodist said—"The Gospel is for the poor and the ignorant," and carried it thither. Unitarians and Universalists declared—"God is one, not three. He damns nobody forever; hates nobody at all. All men shall land in heaven at last, no matter howsoever badly shipwrecked; if they sink, it is to another sea." The Spiritualists say—"The Bible is not a finality; it is no man's master, it is every man's servant. We, as well as the old prophets, can have communion with the departed. Christ reveals himself directly to us, as much as to Paul and Silas, Peter and James."

Now, in all these cases, there was a new idea; not always a true one, but one which stirred men's souls and called forth religious emotions. What energy did religious truths give the followers of Jesus! What power there was in the early Puritans, Baptists, Quakers, Methodists, mixed with folly! Of course, you expect that in all religious movements. What a spread have the doctrines of Universalists and Unitarians had in eighty years! In 1778, I think there were not ten thousand men in all America who believed the distinctive doctrine of Unitarians and Universalists—the ultimate salvation of all men. Now, how wide is the doctrine spread! How rapidly spiritualism has gone abroad; yet it has no great man in its ranks, not a philosopher, not a scholar.

When a great religious idea comes new to any man, what enthusiasm it stirs us to! The followers of Jesus did not comprehend his glorious gospel of piety and morality; they thought more of the man than of his doctrine, his life. They made him a God. "Salvation by Christ" was their creed. The idea was new; and though it was false, it was yet a great improvement over Hebraism and Heathenism of that time. It made a new organization of its own, which covered all Europe with churches. But the vigorous life which once dwelt in the soil of Christendom, and threw up that Ecclesiastical flora, and made those handsome shapes of stone fragrant with the beauty of devotion, it is now all gone. The fossil remains of that religious vegetation tell how mighty the life must have been. What was the state's king before the church's bishop? The Pope put his foot on the neck of emperors, for he had the religion of Christendom to back him. It is not so now, even in Europe. There is no more new religious life in Saint Peter's church at Rome, than in the Pyramids of Egypt. Unburied dead men are in one, buried dead men in the other. So far as new thought is concerned, the Pope is only a mummy.

We want a Revival of Religion in the American church which shall be to this age what the Religion of Jesus was to Heathenism and Judaism, which, though useful once, in his day had served out their time, and had no more that they could do. We do not want a Religion hierarchically organized, which shall generate nothing but meeting-houses made of stone, and end at last in a priesthood. We want a Religion democratically organized, generating great political, social, domestic institutions, and ending in a world full of noble men and women, all their faculties developed well, they serving God with that love which casts out fear.

How can we stir that element to emotions fit for such a work? Only by a Theology which shall meet the people's want, a natural and just idea of man, of God, of the relation between them—of religion, life, duty, destination on earth and in heaven; a theology which has its evidences in the world of matter,—all science, God's testimony thereto; and in the world of consciousness,—every man bearing within him the "lively oracles" the present witnesses of his God, his duty and destination. No sect has such a theology; no great sect aims at such, or the life it leads to. The spiritualists are the only sect that looks forward, and has new fire on its hearth; they alone emancipate themselves from the Bible and the theology of the church, while they also seek to keep the precious truths of the Bible, and all the good things of the church. But even they—I say this modestly; they are a new sect, and everybody wars against them; my criticism I give for their good, in the spirit of hope and tenderness—even they are rapping on coffin lids, listening for ghosts, seeking God and God's truth *beyond* human nature, not *in* human nature. Their religion is Wonder more than Life; not principally addressing itself to the understanding, the imagination, the reason, the conscience, the soul, but to marvelousness more than aught besides. So with many it is amazement, and not elevation. But its function is to destroy the belief in miracles; it will help set many men free from the idols of the old Theologie Den;—no small service, even if it set up new ones of its own; because now they will be less dangerous. I also give thanks for "Spiritualism;" and am not surprised at the follies and extravagances, the dishonesty of "mediums," which I partly see and partly hear of. You must always allow for casualties. You cannot transfer a people from an old Theology to a new one without some breakage and other harm and loss. This is attendant on all human operations. When about to build a meeting-house in the country, of old time, all the town's people came together, on a summer day, for the raising. The village brawler was there, idle boys, loungers, wrestlers, boxers. There was drinking, and swearing now and then. Many got a little hot with liquor. Now and then a spike-pole got crippled, two or three straw hats perished everlastingly. Some brother was overtaken in a fault, and carried home boozy. But they pinned down the ridgepole with shouting; all summer long the building was getting forward, the steeple grew up at last out from the tower; it was rooted in; and in the autumn, there was a harvest of people gathered within its walls, and generation after generation, men went up there for prayers, and holy vows for noble life. Let us always make allowance for casualties, for extravagance, in the old which is fixed, in the new which will become so. What extravagances had the Quakers once, the Christians in Paul's time! I say, we want a Revival of Religion, such as the world has not seen, yet often longed for. It was the dream even of the Hebrew prophets, looking for the time when the nations should learn war no more, when the sword should be turned into the ploughshare, the spear to the pruning-hook, when all men should be taught of God, when "Holiness unto the Lord" should be on the bells even of the horses. We want a Piety so deep that men shall understand God made man from a perfect motive, of perfect material, for a perfect purpose, and endowed with faculties which are perfect means to that end; so deep, that we shall trust the natural law He writes on the body and in the soul. We want a Morality so wide and firm that man shall make the Constitution of the Universe the Common Law of all mankind; every day God's day, a life-time not to be let out to us at the sevenths or the seventieths, the larger fraction for wickedness, the lesser for piety and heaven, but the whole of it His, and the whole of it ours also, because we use it all as He meant it, for our good. Then the dwelling-house, the market-house, the court house, the senate-house, the shop, the ship, the field, the forest, the mine, shall be a temple where the psalm and prayer of Religion goes up from daily, normal, blessed work.

Manly, natural Religion—it is not joining the Church; it is not to believe a creed—Hebrew, Christian, Catholic, Protestant, Trinitarian, Unitarian, Nothingarian. It is not to keep Sunday idle; to attend meeting; to be wet with water; to read the Bible; to offer prayers in words; to take bread and wine in the meeting-house; I know men who do all these things, and yet give scarce more evidence of piety and morality than the benches where they sit,—wood resting on wood. Other men I know who do none of these things, and are yet among the most religious of God's children. Such things may help you—then use them, in God's name, if you find it so. They may hinder,—then, in God's name, cast them off. Jesus of Nazareth was no Christian, in the ecclesiastical sense of that abused word; and could he come to Boston to-day, and bear the same relation to America in the nineteenth century that he did to Palestine in the first, he might not be crucified, or stoned dead in the streets, because the laws forbid such outrage now; but in the "Conference Meeting of Business Men," the prayer meetings of the grimmer sects, the Revivalists, men and women too would beseech God to convert him from the wicked belief that his own religion would save his own soul, that our Father in Heaven was effectually to be served by justice and love to his children; and if God could not do that they would pray—"Remove him out of the way, and let his influence *die with him*." I say those things are not religion; helps or hindrances they may be. Religion itself is something far more inward and living. It is loving God with all your understanding and your heart and soul. It is service of God with every limb of the body, every faculty of the spirit, every power he has given you, every day of your life. That Religion, it is a terror to evil-doers, yet offers them encouragement to repent, it is an inspiration to those who would love man and love God. Suppose I am converted to such a religion; the sunlight of this idea falls on me for the first time, kindling emotions which spring up as the green grass after April rains. What a change will it make in my landscape! Suppose I have kept a drunkery or a brothel. Then I cast off my sin and labor to restore what before I had thrown down, and in cleanness of new life make mankind and myself amends for my past wickedness.

I carry my religion into my daily work, whatever it may be. I am a street-sweeper, then my piety will come out in my faithful performance of duty. No drunkenness, profanity, obscenity, hereafter. The faces of my wife and children will be the certificate of my conversion, of my baptism with the Holy Ghost and with fire. My character will be the sign that I belong to the true Church of God.

I am a young school mistress, perplexed in my business—all young people are, be their business what it may. Then my religion will appear in the discretion, in the sweetness of temper, the forbearance, with which I feed the little unruly flock, and pasture them on learning. I am President of the United States, and this thought of religion comes to me, and I change my wickedness, and seek with my vast powers to do that justice to my brother men which I wish them, with their humble ones, to do to me.

If a minister is filled with this Religion, it will not let him rest. He must speak, whether men hear or whether they forbear. No fear can scare, no bribe can charm, no friends can coax him down. The Church, the State, the World oppose him, all in vain. "Get thee behind me," he quietly says; and while Satan goes from this other son of man in his temptation, angels come and minister to him. He may have small talents; it matters not. The new power of his religious idea comes into him, and one such man "can chase a thousand, and two ten thousand put to flight." Nay, he gets inspiration from God. He makes the axis of his little glass parallel with the axis of God, and the perpendicular Deity shines through with concentrated light and heat.

What if there were one such minister in each of the three hundred and seventy towns of this State—what a Revival would they make in Massachusetts! What an increase of economy, industry, riches! What a growth of temperance, education, justice, love, in all its forms,—a filial, friendly, related, connubial, parental, patriotic, philanthropic love! What if all the thirty thousand Protestant ministers, and the ten thousand Catholic priests, in the United States, had such Religion—worked with such theological ideas of Man, God, duty, destination! There would never be another war, staining America with blood; filibustering would be impossible; political oppression, it would not continue a week; the people would not choose a magistrate in the day time whom they must hire watchers to sit up and look after all night, lest he do mischief; a wicked ruler would be as impossible as a ghost in the day time. Slavery would end before the Fourth of July, and on Independence Day, the Mayor of the city might tell the Rear Admiral of the Turks, "My dear sir, we are converted, and as good as Africans, Mohammedans, and there is not a slave in all the United States. Boston has become almost as Christian as Tunis or Algiers!" What a change would come over the structure of society! Co-operative industry would take the place of selfish antagonism. How would that flower of Womanhood expand with fairer, sweeter, and more prophetic bloom! How would the nation's wealth increase! What Education of all—what Welfare now, what Progress for the future! What a generation of sons and daughters would this people raise up! Aye, what missionaries should we send abroad, not to preach ignorance to the heathen, who have enough of it already, but to carry the light of the Gospel of Life to the nations that "sit in darkness and in the shadows of death!"

Such a Revival of Religion—it is possible; one day it will be actual. The ideal in my heart is a prophecy of the real in mankind's actual life. At length the best must be; this is as sure as that God is Good. But this Revival will not come by miracle. God does his part by creating us with faculties fit for this glorious destination; by providing us, in the material world, the best means to achieve that destination and get this development. To use these powers and opportunities, it is not God's work, it is yours and mine. There never was a miracle, there never will be. Trust me, what God for once makes right, he will never unmake it into wrong.

This Revival of Religion will not come by prayers of words, although the thirty thousand Protestant ministers and the two thousand Catholic priests go down on their knees together. In 1620, our Puritan fathers wished to have all England ploughed up and made fit for farms. Suppose they had gone down on their knees and asked God to do it? Not a furrow would have been turned to-day, not a plough-share forged or cast. A few weeks ago, London men wanted the Great Eastern launched. What if all the English clergy, Episcopal, Dissenters, had put up prayers in the meeting-houses petitioning God to do this work, and the Queen and Parliament had knelt down on their knees in supplication, saying,—"Have mercy upon us, O Lord! miserable offenders. There is no health in us. We beseech Thee to launch her, good Lord!" They might have prayed till they were black in the face, the vessel would not stir an inch. But they used the natural means God gave them. The thinkers prayed great scientific thoughts-—they prayed steam-engines and hydraulic-rams. The laborers prayed work—they prayed with levers and windlasses, and coal-fire. With sore toil, the hydraulic-rams sweat through their iron skin, twelve inches thick. And the launch took place, Mind gave his right arm to Matter, and Miss Leviathan, on her marriage day, coy, timid, reluctant, walked with him to the water, and they became one. Ere long they will take a whole town's population, a wealth of merchandize, and swim the Atlantic together, breast to breast, stroke after stroke, three thousand miles in a week!

Prayer, the devout helpmeet of work, is the brave man's encouragement, when struggling after perfection. But prayer as a substitute for work,—not a wife, to glad the toil and halve the rest, but a witch, to do by magic miracle,—that is blasphemy against the true God—sterile and contemptible.

Ministers talk of a "Revival of Religion in answer to prayer!" It will no more come, than the submarine telegraph from Europe to America. It is the effectual fervent *work* of a righteous man that availeth much—his head-work and hand-work. Gossiping before God, tattling mere words, asking him to do my duty, that is not prayer. I also believe in prayer, from the innermost of my heart, else must I renounce my Manhood and the Godhood above and about me. I also believe in prayer. It is the upspringing of my soul to meet the Eternal, and thereby I seek to alter and improve myself, not Thee, Oh Thou Unchangeable, who art perfect from the beginning! Then I mingle my soul with the Infinite Presence. I am ashamed of my wickedness, my cowardice, sloth, fear. New strength comes unto me of its own accord, as the sunlight to these flowers, which open their little cups. Then I find that he that goeth forth even weeping, bearing this precious seed of prayer, shall doubtless come again rejoicing, and bringing his sheaves with him!

This Revival will not come all at once, as the lightning shineth from the east to the west, but as the morning comes, little by little, so will it be welcomed too. As that material day-spring from on high comes as grateful to grass and trees, to men and women, so will his Revival come upon our hearts, as natural consequence of such prayer and manly toil—our toilsome prayer, our prayerful toil. It will come as the agriculture of New England came—one little field made ready this year, another next—the Indian Corn growing triumphant amid the black stumps of the oaken forest which the axe had hewn down and the fire had swept away, the Savage looking grimly on, no longer meditating war, but yet wondering at the apples which litter the ground with the ruddy loveliness of unwonted, unexpected health. It is coming already:—the peace-men, the temperance-men, anti-slavery men, educational men, the men of science, poetic men, the reform-men, men of commerce, manufactures, agriculture—every good man, every good woman—all these are helps to it, each digging up and planting his little plot of ground. Good ministers of all denominations—Catholic, Protestant, Trinitarian, Unitarian, Methodist, Baptist, Quaker, Universalist, Spiritualist,—there are thousands of them, are toiling after that great end, even though they know it not. Many have done something, some much,—one man more than any. His name is not honored in the *Churches*—of course not! Was Jesus in the Temple? They cast him out even from the synagogue. There is a scholarly man in New England, gifted with such genius for literature as no other American has ever shown. He has large power of intuitive perception of the Beautiful, the True, the Just, the Good, the Holy; cultivated singularly well, having the poetic power of pictured speech, not less than the inward eye to see. His life is heroic as a soldier's; he never runs, nor hides, nor stoops, nor stands aside to avoid the shot which hits tall marks: yet is no woman gentler than this unflinching man. He was cradled in the church—it is good for a cradle, not a college, shop or house. He was bred in the ministry, and sat at famous feet. The little town of Concord is the center of his sphere; its circumference,—that great circle lies far off, hid underneath the foreign horizon of future centuries.

I honor the Chaunceys, the Mayhews, the Freemans, the Buckminsters, the Channings, who taught great truths, and also lived full of nobleness; I thank God for their words, which come directly, or echoed, to your heart and mine. They have gone to their reward. But no living man has done so much as Emerson to waken this Religion in the great Saxon heart of Americans and Britons. It is not doctrine he teaches—his own creed is not well defined; it is the inspiration of manliness that he imparts. He has never beguiled a man or unsuspecting maid to join a church to underwrite another's creed, or comply with an alien ritual. But his words and his life charm earnest men with such natural religion as makes them, of their own accord, to trust the Great Soul of all, and refine themselves into noble, normal, individual life. In six hours of so many recent weeks, I think he has done more to promote the revival of Piety and Morality in Boston, than all the noisy rant of Calvinistic preaching, Calvinistic singing, and Calvinistic prayer, in the last six months.

What an opportunity there is for you and me to work in this true Revival! No nation offers a field so fair. We can speak and listen, we can print and read, with none to molest or make us afraid. More than all that, we can live as high as we please. There is no government, no church, to lay its iron hands on our heads and say—"Stop there!" Misguiding ministers may believe in the damnation of babies newly born, may pray curses on us all; they cannot light a faggot to burn a man. Their spirit is willing, but their flesh is weak! It is a grand age and nation to live in and work for.

The first thing that you and I want is to be religious in this sense—to know the Infinite God, who is perfect Power, perfect Wisdom, perfect Justice, perfect Holiness, and perfect Love. Knowing Him, you cannot fail to love with your understanding and your heart, to love His world about us, within us, and all His laws. The warmth and moisture of the ground, they come out in the grass and in the trees, in the beauty and the fragrance of these violets, in this rose which, "beside his sweetness, is a cure;" and so your and my piety must blossom in our service of God with every limb of this body, every faculty of this spirit—the normal use of every power and opportunity we have, Sundays, Mondays, all time.

Then daily work shall be a gospel, life our continual transfiguration to a nobler growth. We shall bless our town, our nation, our age, our race. When we die, we shall leave the world better because we have lived, with more Welfare now, fitter for Progress hereafter. We shall bear away with us the triumphant result of every trial, every duty, every effort, every tear, every prayer, every suffering, nay, the great longing aspiration after excellence. And there and then the motherly hand of God shall be reached out over us, and we shall hear the blessed word—"Come, my beloved, thou hast been faithful over a few things; I will make thee ruler over many things. Enter thou into thy Mother's joy!"

Notes

INTRODUCTION

1. William G. McLoughlin, *The Meaning of Henry Ward Beecher* (New York: Knopf, 1970), p. 254.

2. Henry Steele Commager, *Theodore Parker: Yankee Crusader* (Boston: Little, Brown and Company, 1936), p. 287.

3. Robert C. Albrecht, *Theodore Parker* (New York: Twayne Publishers, 1971), p. 60.

4. John White Chadwick, *Theodore Parker: Preacher and Reformer* (Boston: Houghton Mifflin Company, 1900), p. 285.

5. John Weiss, *Life and Correspondence of Theodore Parker* (New York: D. Appleton and Company, 1864), p. 2:42. Chadwick's two-volume work is an excellent source of the correspondence to and from Parker.

6. Chadwick, *Theodore Parker: Preacher and Reformer*, pp. 150, 165–66.

7. Theodore Parker, *Centenary Edition of the Works of Theodore Parker*, edited and with notes by Rufus Leighton (Boston: American Unitarian Association, 1907–1910), pp. 8:19–20.

CHAPTER 1: PROLOGUE: A MID-NINETEENTH-CENTURY PREACHER

1. Gaius Glen Atkins, ed., *Master Sermons of the Nineteenth Century* (New York: Harper & Brothers, 1940), p. ix.

2. Ibid., p. x.

3. Roy C. McCall, "Theodore Parker," *A History and Criticism of American Public Address*, William Norwood Brigance, ed. (New York: Russell & Russell, 1960), p. 1:238.

4. Henry Steele Commager, *Theodore Parker: Yankee Crusader* (Boston: Little Brown, and Company, 1836), p. 255. Commager adds that "only Horace Greeley was more widely read" than Parker.

5. Theodore Parker, *Theodore Parker's Experience as a Minister* (Boston: Rufus Leighton Jr., 1859), pp. 101–102.

6. John White Chadwick, *Theodore Parker: Preacher and Reformer* (Boston: Houghton Mifflin and Company, 1900), p. 355.

7. Parker, *Experience as a Minister*, p. 103.

8. Paxton Hibben, *Henry Ward Beecher: An American Portrait* (New York: Beekman Publishers, Inc., 1974; repr. of 1942 ed.), pp. xiii–xiv.

9. As quoted in Commager, *Theodore Parker: Yankee Crusader*, p. 115.

10. Theodore Parker, *Centenary Edition of the Works of Theodore Parker* (Boston: American Unitarian Association, 1907–1910), pp. 8:19–20.

11. Parker, *Centenary Edition*, p. 13:304.

12. McCall, "Theodore Parker," p. 1:240.

CHAPTER 2: THE EARLY YEARS (1810–1841)

1. As quoted in John White Chadwick, *Theodore Parker: Preacher and Reformer* (Boston: Houghton Mifflin Company, 1900), p. 5.

2. Theodore Parker, *Centenary Edition of the Works of Theodore Parker*, edited and with notes by Rufus Leighton (Boston: American Unitarian Association, 1907–1910), pp. 13:11–12.

3. Ibid., pp. 15–16.

4. John Weiss, *Life and Correspondence of Theodore Parker* (New York: D. Appleton & Company, 1864), p. 1:30.

5. Donald S. Harrington, "Theodore Parker, Crusader," *The Rhetorical Tradition: Principles and Practice*, David Ross Chandler, ed. (Boston: Kendall/Hunt Publishing Company, 1978), p. 159.

6. Chadwick, *Theodore Parker: Preacher and Reformer*, p. 26.

7. Ibid., pp. 25–26.

8. Ibid., p. 32.

9. Henry Steele Commager, *Theodore Parker: Yankee Crusader* (Boston: Little, Brown and Company, 1936), p. 28. When Ware's father was appointed to the Hollis Professorship at Harvard in 1805, it marked the turn of the college to Unitarianism as its philosophical and religious foundation.

10. Ibid., p. 30.

11. Ibid., p. 31.

12. Weiss, *Life and Correspondence of Theodore Parker*, pp.1:66–67.

13. Chadwick, *Theodore Parker: Preacher and Reformer*, p. 39.

14. Weiss, *Life and Correspondence of Theodore Parker*, pp. 1:70–71.

15. Ibid., p. 86.

16. Ibid., p. 91.

17. Commager, *Theodore Parker: Yankee Crusader*, p. 37.

18. Weiss, *Life and Correspondence of Theodore Parker*, p. 1:94.

19. Chadwick, *Theodore Parker: Preacher and Reformer*, p. 51.

20. Weiss, *Life and Correspondence of Theodore Parker*, pp. 1:94–95.

21. Commager, *Theodore Parker: Yankee Crusader*, p. 38.

22. Chadwick, *Theodore Parker: Preacher and Reformer*, p. 60.

23. Ibid.

24. Weiss, *Life and Correspondence of Theodore Parker*, p. 1:113.

25. William R. Hutchinson, *The Transcendental Ministers: Church Reform in the New England Renaissance* (New Haven: Yale University Press, 1959), pp. vii, viii.

26. Henry Steele Commager, ed., *Theodore Parker: An Anthology* (Boston: Beacon Press, 1960), pp. 89–90.

27. Ibid., p. 90.

28. Ibid., p. 93.

29. Ibid., p. 94.

30. Ibid.

31. Ibid., p. 95.

32. Perry Miller, *The Transcendentalists: An Anthology* (Cambridge: Harvard University Press, 1950), p. 226.

33. Commager, *Theodore Parker: An Anthology*, pp. 96–97.

34. Sydney E. Ahlstrom, ed., *Theology in America: The Major Protestant Voices From Puritanism to Neo-Orthodoxy* (Indianapolis: Bobbs-Merrill Co., 1967), p. 208.

35. Ahlstrom, *A Religious History of the American People* (New Haven: Yale University Press, 1971), p. 402.

36. Commager, *Theodore Parker: Yankee Crusader*, p. 62.

37. Chadwick, *Theodore Parker: Preacher and Reformer*, p. 125. Channing was sixty-two years old when he died.

38. Commager, *Theodore Parker: Yankee Crusader*, p. 78.

39. Theodore Parker, *Theodore Parker's Experience as a Minister* (Boston: Rufus Leighton Jr., 1859), pp. 45–46.

40. Chadwick, *Theodore Parker: Preacher and Reformer*, pp. 63, 64.

41. Parker, *Experience as a Minister*, pp. 46, 48–49.

42. Theodore Parker, *West Roxbury Sermons by Theodore Parker, 1837–1838*, edited and with an introduction by Samuel J. Barrows (Boston: Roberts Brothers, 1892), p. 1.

43. Ibid., pp. 28–29.

44. Ibid., pp. 31–42.

45. Ibid., pp. 48–49.

46. Ibid., pp. 74, 75, 78–79, 81–82, 85.

47. Ibid., pp. 89–104.

48. Ibid., pp. 131–32.

49. Ibid., pp. 197, 205–206, 207–208.

50. Ibid., pp. 216–35.

51. Parker, *Centenary Edition*, p. 13:viii.

52. Chadwick, *Theodore Parker: Preacher and Reformer*, p. 150.

53. Weiss, *Life and Correspondence of Theodore Parker*, p. 1:111.

54. Robert T. Oliver, *History of Public Speaking in America* (Boston: Allyn and Bacon, 1965), p. 371.

55. Parker, *Centenary Edition*, pp. 13:398–99.

CHAPTER 3: THE YEARS OF INFLUENCE (1841–1859)

1. Roy C. McCall, "Theodore Parker," *A History and Criticism of American Public Address*, William Norwood Brigance, ed. (New York: Russell & Russell, 1960), p. 1:242.

2. John White Chadwick, *Theodore Parker: Preacher and Reformer* (Boston: Houghton Mifflin Company, 1900), pp. 52, 71.

3. Henry Steele Commager, *Theodore Parker: Yankee Crusader* (Boston: Little, Brown and Company, 1936), p. 123.

4. McCall, "Theodore Parker," p. 1:240.

5. Chadwick, *Theodore Parker: Preacher and Reformer*, p. 56.

6. Commager, *Theodore Parker: Yankee Crusader*, p. 129.

7. *Richmond Examiner* (Virginia), November 6, 1842.

8. *Streeter's Weekly Boston Star*, April 11, 1846.

9. McCall, "Theodore Parker," p. 1:245.

10. Theodore Parker, *Centenary Edition of the Works of Theodore Parker* (Boston: American Unitarian Association, 1907–1910), p. 13:352.

11. McCall, "Theodore Parker," p. 1:245.

12. James Freeman Clark, *A Look at the Life of Theodore Parker* (Boston: George H. Ellis Company, 1910). This was a speech delivered on June 3, 1880.

13. Parker, *Centenary Edition*, pp. 8:95–96.

14. Ibid., p. 160.

15. Ibid., p. 7:246.

16. Ibid., p. 8:435. Words of admiration were dominant in the article. "Beecher has great strength of instinct, of spontaneous human feeling. . . . A mountain spring supplies Mr. Beecher with fresh, living water. . . . He has great fellow-feeling with the joys and sorrows of men. Hence he is always on the side of suffering, especially of the oppressed; all his sermons and lectures indicate this. . . . A great-hearted, eloquent, live-man, full of religious emotion, of humanity and love,—no wonder he is dear to the people of America." pp. 427, 437.

17. McCall, "Theodore Parker," p. 1:252.

18. Theodore Parker, *The Moral Condition of Boston* (Boston: Crosby and Nichols, 1849), pp. 15–16. An example of Parker's use of statistics in this sermon was his report on crime in Boston. "In 1848, 3,435 grown persons, and 671 minors were lawfully sentenced in your Jail and House of Corrections; in all 4,106; 3,444 persons were arrested by the night police, and 11,178 were taken into custody by the watch; at one time there were 144 in the common jail." p. 18.

19. McCall, "Theodore Parker," p. 1:252.

20. Peter Dean, *The Life and Teachings of Theodore Parker* (London: William and Norgate, Ltd., 1877), p. 144.

21. John Weiss, *Life and Correspondence of Theodore Parker* (New York: D. Appleton & Company, 1864), p. 1:340.

22. McCall, "Theodore Parker," p. 1:246.

23. Ibid., p. 262.

24. Theodore Parker, "The Transient and Permanent in Christianity," *The Critical and Miscellaneous Writings of Theodore Parker* (Boston: J. Munroe and Co., 1843), pp. 126–57.

25. Daniel Ross Chandler, "Theodore Parker (1810–1860), Unitarian Clergyman," *American Orators Before 1900: Critical Studies and Sources*, Bernard K. Duffy and Halford R. Ryan, eds. (Westport, CT: Greenwood Press, 1987), p. 308.

26. William R. Hutchinson, *The Transcendental Ministers: Church Reform in the New England Renaissance* (New Haven: Yale University Press, 1959), p. 98.

27. Commager, *Theodore Parker: Yankee Crusader*, p. 76.

28. As quoted in Hutchinson, *The Transcendental Ministers*, p. 114.

29. Commager, *Theodore Parker: Yankee Crusader*, pp. 76–77.

30. Weiss, *Life and Correspondence of Theodore Parker*, p. 1:177.

31. Parker, *Centenary Edition*, pp. 1:341, 10–11.

32. As quoted in Hutchinson, *The Transcendental Ministers*, pp. 104–105.

33. Parker, *Centenary Edition*, pp. 1:364, 433, 435.

34. Theodore Parker, *A Discourse of Matters Pertaining to Religion* (Boston: Charles C. Little and James Brown, 1842), pp. 429–34.

35. Ibid., pp. 456–59.

36. Ibid., p. 473.

37. Parker, *Centenary Edition*, p. 1:258.

38. Ibid., p. 259.

39. Commager, *Theodore Parker: Yankee Crusader*, p. 270.

40. Ibid., p. 89.

41. Ibid., pp. 89–90.

42. Daniel Ross Chandler, "Theodore Parker," p. 309.

43. Commager, *Theodore Parker: Yankee Crusader*, pp. vii–viii.

44. Fred Gladstone Bratton, *The Legacy of the Liberal Spirit* (New York: Charles Scribner's Sons, 1943), p. 170.

45. Parker, *Centenary Edition*, pp. 13:27–28, 42–43.

46. Bratton, *The Legacy of the Liberal Spirit*, p. 169.

47. Theodore Parker, *Centenary Edition*, pp. 8:178–79.

48. Ibid., p. 13:94.

49. Oscar Sherwin, *Prophet of Liberty: The Life and Times of Wendell Phillips* (New York: Bookman Associates, 1958), pp. 410–11.

50. Parker, *Centenary Edition*, pp. 9:9–10.

51. "A Sermon of Merchants," *The Transcendentalists: An Anthology*, Perry Miller, ed. (Cambridge: Harvard University Press, 1950), pp. 450–51.

52. Ibid., p. 451.

53. Ibid.

54. Ibid., pp. 451, 452.

55. Ibid., pp. 454–55.

56. Ibid., pp. 455–57.

57. Parker, *The Public Education of the People* (Boston: Wm Crosby & H. P. Nichols, 1850), p. 3.

58. Ibid., pp. 13–16.

59. Ibid., pp. 20, 41.

60. Ibid., p. 45.

61. Ibid., pp. 32–33.

62. Ibid., pp. 34–35.

63. Ibid., p. 38.

64. Ibid., p. 40.

65. Ibid., p. 44.

66. Ibid., p. 48.

67. Ibid., p. 53.

68. Ibid., p. 57.

69. Parker, *Centenary Edition*, p. 11:5.

70. Ibid., pp. 6, 13.

71. Ibid., p. 22.

72. Ibid., p. 21.

73. Ibid., p. 29.

74. Ibid., p. 200.

75. Ibid., pp. 254–55.

76. Ibid., p. 248.

77. Ibid., p. 201.

78. Ibid., p. 203.

79. Ibid., p. 10.

80. Ibid., p. 304.

81. Ibid., p. 9:44.

82. John Weiss, *Life and Correspondence of Theodore Parker,* pp. 2:99–100.

83. Parker, *Centenary Edition,* p. 9:20.

84. Ibid., p. 11:337.

85. Ibid., p. 9:47.

86. Ibid., pp. 11:322–23.

87. Ibid., pp. 219-20, 241, 243.

88. Ibid., pp. 7:352, 367, 371.

89. Robert T. Oliver, *History of Public Speaking in America* (Boston: Allyn and Bacon, Inc., 1965), pp. 372–73.

90. Commager, *Theodore Parker: Yankee Crusader,* p. 231.

91. Parker, *Centenary Edition,* pp. 11:292, 311.

92. Commager, *Theodore Parker: Yankee Crusader,* p. 208.

93. Parker, *Centenary Edition,* p. 9:63.

94. Ibid., p. 11:340.

95. Ibid., p. 9:33.

96. Ibid., p. 11:185.

97. Ibid., p. 279.

98. Ibid., p. 188.

99. Chester Forrester Dunham, *The Attitude of the Northern Clergy Toward the South, 1860–1865* (Philadelphia: Porcupine Press, 1974), p. 82.

100. Parker, *Centenary Edition,* pp. 11:205–206.

101. Ibid., p. 9:87.

102. Commager, *Theodore Parker: Yankee Crusader,* p. 197.

103. Dunham, *The Attitude of the Northern Clergy,* p. 38.

104. Parker, *Centenary Edition,* p. 11:181.

105. Ibid., p. 37.

106. Ibid., pp. 9:19–20.

107. Ibid., p. 291.

108. Ibid., p. 298.

109. Ibid., p. 11:173.

110. Ibid., p. 251.

111. Ibid., p. 9:44.

112. Commager, *Theodore Parker: Yankee Crusader,* p. 215.

113. Chadwick, *Theodore Parker: Preacher and Reformer,* p. 355.

114. Weiss, *Life and Correspondence of Theodore Parker,* pp. 2:170–71.

115. Sydney E. Ahlstrom, *A Religious History of the American People* (New Haven: Yale University Press, 1972), p. 738.

116. Oliver, *History of Public Speaking in America,* p. 384.

117. Marie Hochmuth and Norman W. Mattis, "Phillips Brooks," *History and*

Criticism of American Public Address, William Norwood Brigance, ed. (New York: Russell & Russell, 1960), p. 1:310.

118. "Of the 814 numbered sermons Brooks is known to have written, approximately two-thirds remain; slightly more than 400 of these are in manuscript form in the Houghton Library in Harvard University, 200 are to be found in ten volumes of his sermons, and others have been widely scattered or lost. In addition to the full length manuscript sermons the Houghton Library has 585 outlines, work sheets and lecture notes." Raymond Albright, *Focus on Infinity* (New York: The Macmillan Company, 1961), p. viii.

119. Theodore Parker, *Historic Americans* (London: Trubner & Co., 1871), pp. 49–57.

120. Ibid., pp. 109–10, 113.

121. Ibid., pp. 223, 225–26.

122. Theodore Parker, *Speeches, Addresses, and Occasional Sermons* (Boston: Horace B. Fuller, 1871), pp. 2:281–82.

123. Ibid., pp. 283–84.

124. Ibid., p. 298.

125. Ibid., p. 300.

126. Ibid., p. 271.

127. Ibid., p. 273.

128. Ibid., p. 275.

129. Ibid., pp. 277–78.

130. Ibid., p. 301.

131. Ibid., pp. 325–26.

132. Ibid., pp. 303–305.

133. Ibid., pp. 308–309.

134. Ibid., pp. 328–29.

135. Parker's journal contains his long-range sermon/lecture plans for 1845–1846.

Scheme of Lectures for 1845–1846

1. History of the growth of the Roman Hierarchy till 1517
2. History of the growth of the Roman Dogmatics till 1517
3. State of Europe—1511 Polit. not phil. moral, rel.
4. Formation of a power hostile to the hierarchy and dogmatics of the R. C.
5. The Reformation—Antagonistic to the R. C.
6. The Church's defense—Loyola
7. Luther: The threefold division of the Ref. movement
8. Calvin
9. Swingli
10. Political consequences of the Ref.
11. The moral and intellectual consequences-effects, etc.
12. The Catholic Ref—Council of Trent
    Develop this further as I have time & give the life of Erasmus, Melancthon, etc.
    As recorded in McCall, "Theodore Parker," pp. 1:244–45.

136. Theodore Parker, *The Biblical, the Ecclesiastical, and the Philosophical Notion*

118   *Notes*

of God, and the Soul's Delight in Him (New York: John F. Trow, 1858), pp. 41, 42, 44.

137. As recorded in Commager, *Theodore Parker: Yankee Crusader*, p. 119.

138. Parker, *Centenary Edition*, p. 13:258.

139. *Prayers by Theodore Parker*, A new edition with a preface by Louisa M. Alcott, and a memoir by F. B. Sanborn (Boston: Roberts Brothers, 1882), pp. iii–iv.

140. Oliver, *History of Public Speaking in America*, p. 369.

141. McCall, "Theodore Parker," p. 1:249.

142. Commager, *Theodore Parker: Yankee Crusader*, p. 32.

143. Theodore Parker, *Discourse of Matters Pertaining to Religion*, pp. 22–23.

144. McCall, "Theodore Parker," p. 1:258.

145. Parker, *Centenary Edition*, 8:17–18.

146. Ibid., 7:336–37.

147. Ibid., p. 338.

148. Ibid., 8:420.

149. Beecher was a ground-breaker in the deliberate use of humor from the pulpit. Frederick Douglass was another nineteenth-century orator who used humor with great affect.

150. McCall, "Theodore Parker," p. 1:260.

151. Oliver, *History of Public Speaking in America*, p. 371.

152. As noted in Chadwick, *Theodore Parker: Preacher and Reformer*, p. 217.

153. Perry Miller, ed., *The Transcendentalists: An Anthology*, p. 502.

154. James Russell Lowell, *A Fable For Critics* (Freeport, NY: Books for Libraries Press, 1972; repr. of 1890 ed.), pp. 101–102.

155. Oliver, *History of Public Speaking in America*, p. 371.

156. As quoted in McCall, "Theodore Parker," p. 1:258.

157. William J. Herndon and Jessie William Weik, *Herndon's Lincoln* (Springfield, IL: W. H. Herndon Publishing Company, 1921), p. 3:445. Commager has written of the friendship between Parker and William Herndon. "He [Herndon] was always stumbling . . . upon some great truths, and confiding his discoveries to Parker. . . . He told everything to Parker, letter after letter . . . he was so anxious to show him how deeply he thought about things. . . . It was from Herndon that Parker learned all about Illinois Politics, about Lyman Trumbull and Abraham Lincoln. . . . And it was Herndon who advertised the fame of Parker, spread his ideas . . . over the State, pressed his sermons and speeches on his friends" [including Lincoln]. Commager, *Theodore Parker: Yankee Crusader*, p. 262.

158. Herndon and Weik, *Herndon's Lincoln*, p. 2:396.

159. Parker, *Centenary Edition*, p. 6:30.

160. Garry Wills, *Lincoln at Gettysburg: The Words That Remade America* (New York: Simon & Schuster, 1992), p. 107. For further commentary on Parker's use of this refrain, see Chadwick, *Theodore Parker: Preacher and Reformer*, pp. 322–23.

161. Roy P. Basler, ed., *The Collected Works of Abraham Lincoln* (New Brunswick, NJ: Rutgers University Press, 1953), p. 2:452.

162. James M. McPherson, *Abraham Lincoln and the Second American Revolution* (New York: Oxford University Press, 1991), p. 104.

163. As quoted in Dunham, *The Attitude of the Northern Clergy*, p. 38.

164. Taylor Branch, *Parting the Waters: America in the King Years, 1954–1963* (New York: Simon & Schuster, 1988), p. 197. See also, Martin Luther King Jr., *A Testament of Hope: The Essential Writings of Martin Luther King Jr.*, James M.

Washington, ed. (San Francisco: Harper & Row, 1986), p. 88.

165. Lane Cooper, *The Rhetoric of Aristotle: An Expanded Translation With Supplementary Examples For Students of Composition and Public Speaking* (New York: Appleton-Century-Crofts, Inc., 1932), p. 9.

166. David Ross Chandler, "Theodore Parker (1810–1860), Unitarian Clergyman," p. 310.

167. Thomas B. Reed, *Modern Eloquence* (Philadelphia: John D. Morris, 1900), p. 1:256.

168. Ibid., p. 8:797.

CHAPTER 4: THE WANING MONTHS (1859–1860)

1. As quoted in Donald S. Harrington, "Theodore Parker, Crusader," *The Rhetorical Tradition: Principles and Practice*, Daniel Ross Chandler, ed. (Boston: Kendall/Hunt Publishing Company, 1978), p. 166.

2. John Weiss, *Life and Correspondence of Theodore Parker* (New York: D. Appleton and Company, 1864), p. 2:256.

3. Ibid., pp. 256–57.

4. Ibid., p. 265.

5. As quoted in John White Chadwick, *Theodore Parker: Preacher and Reformer* (Boston: Houghton, Mifflin and Company, 1900), p. 353.

6. Theodore Parker, *Theodore Parker's Experience as a Minister* (Boston: Rufus Leighton, Jr., 1859), p. 176. Henry Steel Commager made the following appraisal of Parker's struggle against slavery. "Too much of his energy had gone into the fight against slavery; that had come to overshadow everything else in his life, it had deflected him from scholarship and even from social reform; it had wrecked his plans. . . . It was not, in itself, more important than spiritual or social reform, but he came to realize that nothing could be effected until this question of slavery had been settled, and settled right. He came to see that you couldn't emancipate the minds of men until you had emancipated their bodies, that you couldn't advance the cause of free labor until you had done away with slave labor." Henry Steele Commager, *Theodore Parker: Yankee Crusader* (Boston: Little, Brown and Company, 1936), pp. 292–93.

7. Parker, *Experience As A Minister*, pp. 117, 118, 119, 123, 127, 134, 136, 141.

8. Chadwick, *Theodore Parker: Preacher and Reformer*, p. 358.

9. Parker was right in his concern. The Twenty-eighth Congregational Society slowly withered away without its leader. In 1863 the congregation abdicated the spacious Music Hall and returned to the Melodeon. A few years later the Society moved to even smaller quarters, and in 1889, too small to further sustain itself, officially disbanded. Daniel Ross Chandler, "Theodore Parker (1810–1860), Unitarian Clergyman," *American Orators Before 1900: Critical Studies and Sources*, Bernard K. Duffy and Halford R. Ryan, eds. (Westport, CT: Greenwood Press, 1987), p. 311.

10. John Weiss, *Life and Correspondence of Theodore Parker*, pp. 2:376–77.

11. Ibid., p. 178.

12. Ibid., p. 408.

13. Chadwick, *Theodore Parker: Preacher and Reformer*, p. 370.

14. Commager, *Theodore Parker: Yankee Crusader*, p. 308.

15. Chadwick, *Theodore Parker: Preacher and Reformer*, p. 371.

16. Fred Gladstone Bratton, *The Legacy of the Liberal Spirit* (New York: Charles

Scribner's Sons, 1943), p. 182.

17. Philip S. Foner, ed., *The Life and Writings of Frederick Douglass* (New York: International Publishers, 1950), pp. 4:126–27.

18. Chadwick, *Theodore Parker: Preacher and Reformer*, p. 384.

Chronology of Selected Speeches

Some of Parker's most significant sermons/speeches are listed below. Most of them have been referred to in the preceding text.

1841

January 31   "A Sermon of Slavery." This was Parker's first antislavery sermon. In it he sought to demolish the arguments of Northerners who claimed that slavery was not their concern.

May 19   "The Transient and Permanent in Christianity." This sermon, probably Parker's best known, was preached at Dawes Place Church in Boston during the ordination service of C. C. Shackford. Parker used this occasion to challenge and dispute orthodox theology.

1846

January   "The True Idea Of the Christian Church." This sermon was delivered at Parker's installation as the pastor of the Twenty-eighth Congregational Society on the first Sunday of January. Parker shared his vision of what a true church should be.

June 7   "A Sermon Of War." In response to the Mexican War, Parker charged that "war is a violation of Christianity. . . . [War] is a national infidelity, a denial of Christianity and God." This was not a position that Parker would later advocate when the probability of a civil war was on the horizon.

August 30   "The Perishing Classes of Boston." In this sermon, delivered at the Melodeon, Parker drew a vivid description of what it meant to be poor in Boston, and urged solutions to poverty. "All that is lacking is the prudent will," he exclaimed.

November 30   "A Sermon Of Merchants." At the Melodeon, Parker delivered a sermon wherein he laid much of the blame for society's ills on the merchant class who controlled society, even the churches, for the sake of its own profits. The widely publicized sermon created a great sensation throughout Boston.

1847

January 31   "The Dangerous Classes in Society." In this sermon, delivered at the Melodeon, Parker announced that there were two types of criminals in society. There were criminals who are the victims of society, those who do evil because their circumstances are evil; and there are those criminals who are born the foes of society. "The cause of their crime is in their bodily constitution itself." This latter group poses the greatest dangers to society and are often found among the social elites.

1848

March 5   "A Discourse Occasioned by the Death of John Quincy Adams." In a lengthy sermon, even by Parker's standards, Parker praised the memory of his friend and former President of the United States. Though specifically acknowledging some of Adams' faults, Parker proclaimed that Adams had "an intense love of freedom for all men." He concluded by declaring that Adams was "the one great man since Washington, whom America had no cause to fear."

1849

February 4   "The Mexican War." In an address delivered at Faneuil Hall in Boston, as federal troops with bayonets looked on, Parker denounced the Mexican War. "This war is waged for a mean and infamous purpose, for the extension of slavery. . . . Your President tells you it is treason to talk so! . . . If my country is in the wrong, and I know it, and hold my peace, then I am guilty of treason, moral treason."

February 11   "A Sermon on the Moral Condition of Boston."
This sermon, delivered at the Melodeon, was a strong indictment of Boston as an immoral city. Parker singles out the immorality of trade, commerce, and the press for special attention. He deplored the existence of poverty, crime, and the sale of intoxicating beverages.

February 18   "A Sermon on the Spiritual Condition of Boston."
On the Sunday following his sermon on the moral condition of Boston, Parker, at the Melodeon, delivered a sermon on the spiritual condition of the city. Declaring that piety in moral action was more important than ecclesiastical piety, Parker was more hopeful about the present than the past.

October 4   "The Public Education of the People." In this address before the Teachers' Institute, in Syracuse, New York, Parker affirmed that "the democratic State has never done its political and educational duty, until it affords every man a chance to obtain the greatest amount of education." Parker called for "free common schools," "free high schools," and "free colleges." He strongly denounced those groups and practices in America that stood in the way of full public education.

1850

March 25   "Discourse on Webster." At Faneuil Hall, Parker strongly condemned Daniel Webster for the Senator's role in the passage of the Fugitive Slave Law. "He has done wrong things before, cowardly things more than once; but this, the wrongest and most cowardly of them all, we did not look for. . . . I know of no deed in American history, done by a son of New England, to which I can compare this, but the act of Benedict Arnold."

September 22 "The Function and Place of Conscience in Relation to the Laws of Man." In this sermon at the Melodeon, Parker developed the concept of higher law (conscience) and how it is a person's duty to obey it above all other demands. He applied this specifically to the Fugitive Slave Law, declaring that higher law called people to disobey this lower and evil law.

November 28   "The State of the Nation." In this Thanksgiving sermon, at the Melodeon, Parker depicted major differences between the North and South, demonstrating the South to be an inferior culture to the North.

1851

April 10   "The Chief Sins of the People." At the Melodeon, Parker declared that the desire for wealth was America's chief sin. Money interests controlled most churches, cooperated with the slave power of the South, and supported the Fugitive Slave Law. Much of the sermon is a harsh denunciation of that law and of Boston's cooperation with it.

1852

April 12   "The Boston Kidnapping." At the Melodeon, on the first anniversary of Boston returning a fugitive slave, Thomas Sims, to the South, Parker poignantly pictured Sims' despair in being forced to return to slavery. This sermon is an example of Parker's prose at its most dramatic and eloquent best.

October 31   "A Discourse Occasioned by the Death of Daniel Webster." At the Melodeon, Parker declared that his mourning for Webster began long before the Senator's death; when Webster made speeches and supported legislation that betrayed the slaves. Though some, such as Julia Ward Howe, praised Parker's words, others condemned him for speaking ill of the dead.

1853

March 27   "The Public Function of Women." In this sermon on the role of women in society, at the Music Hall, Parker's words demonstrated that he was both a progressive and somewhat a child of his times. "When she is recognized as the equivalent of man in her individual, social, political, domestic and ecclesiastical rights, most beautiful results will follow." There were no reasons why a woman "should not be a voter and hold office and administer laws," but Parker doubted "that she will ever take the same interest as men in political affairs, or find there an abiding satisfaction."

1854

February 12   "The Nebraska Question: Some Thoughts on the Assault Upon Freedom in America." At the Music Hall, Parker spoke of the Congressional debate on granting the Nebraska territory the right to decide by popular vote if it would or would not be a slave state. He declared that "it is an attempt by the Federal Government to establish it [slavery] in a territory where it has been prohibited by the Federal government itself, by the solemn enactment of Congress, more that thirty-three years ago, at a time when all the North swore solemnly that it would not suffer slavery to come North another inch."

June 18   "The Law of God and the Statutes of Men." In a sermon at the Music Hall, Parker returned to a central theme in his preaching. The human conscience transfers "the Moral Ideal . . . from God's mind to our mind." This is the highest law, the Law of God. When Higher Law conflicts with ecclesiastical creeds and/or legal statutes, it is Higher Law that is to be obeyed, and the lower laws disobeyed. The conscience, both individual and collective, is enlightened in stages (progressively). "We learn the Law of our moral nature like the Laws of matter, slowly, little by little." This sermon is a prime example of Parker's organizational skills and his use of historical and biblical illustrations.

July 2   "A Sermon of the Dangers Which Threaten the Rights of Man in America." In observance of Independence Day, at the Music Hall, Parker, after a historical analysis depicting the fall of other nations, declared that American "success was never so doubtful as at this time." He spoke of four great perils threatening the nation: (1) devotion to riches, (2) the Roman Catholic Church, (3) the failure to recognize higher law, and (4) the institution of slavery.

July 11   "The Dangers From Slavery." In this sermon Parker used the "house-divided" metaphor, four years before Lincoln's famous "house-divided" speech. Evidence suggests that Lincoln borrowed this figure of speech from Parker.

November 5   "Moral Dangers Incident To Prosperity." At the Music Hall, Parker declared that "prosperity is not a good schoolmaster to produce the higher forms of character." Drawing numerous examples from individual and social history, Parker emphasized that "excessive prosperity was of great peril to . . . moral character." "The best age of the Christian Church," he noted, "was when all the world opposed her."

November 21   "Consequences of an Immoral Principle and False Ideas of Life." At the Music Hall, Parker declared that evil was "abnormal," thus affirming his faith in the goodness and potentiality of human kind.

Yet, he saw signs of a spreading abnormality in America. These offenses, "committed by persons of high standing in society," fell into three classes: (1) offenses against the property of individuals, (2) offenses against the life of individuals, and (3) offenses against the property and life of other nations. Under each class, Parker gave specific recent examples and called out the names of specific violators. He warned, "God is not mocked; whatsoever a man soweth, that shall he also reap."

1855

May 7   "The Great Battle of Slavery and Freedom." In this address before the American Antislavery Society in New York City, Parker debated the question of whether slavery or freedom would take over the territories. "Shall Slavery spread over all the United States, and root out Freedom from the land? or shall Freedom spread wide her blessed boughs till the whole continent is fed by her fruit, and lodged beneath her arms,—her very leaves for the healing of the nations? That is the ultimate question."

1856

May 25   "A New Lesson For the Day." At the Music Hall, Parker began this sermon by denouncing the despotism in Russia for the attack on Turkey. He then denounced the slave despotism in America. He spoke of the beating of Charles Sumner on the Senate floor, declaring that it was indicative of the violent spirit of slavery. Parker strongly scolded those in the North who cooperated with such despotism. He paid special attention to judges who ordered the return of fugitive slaves.

1858

January 29   "The Present Aspect of Slavery in America and the Immediate Duty of the North." This speech was delivered before the Massachusetts Anti-Slavery Convention at the Hall of the State House in Boston. Parker accused the "Slave Power" of controlling the Federal Government with much support from the great northern cities of Cincinnati, Philadelphia, New York, and Boston. Though slavery was still gaining in power (Parker gave several examples) he drew hope because of new challenges to slavery. He urged the young Republican party to nominate a presidential candidate in 1860 who would not compromise with slavery. He noted that Webster and Clay had compromised and failed, and urged the Republicans to closely examine the credentials of Seward, Chase, and Banks.

April 4   "A False and True Revival of Religion." At the Music Hall, Parker denounced popular religious revival wherein people become passionate about particular doctrinal beliefs. Such a revival often leads to injustices upon those who do not hold similar beliefs. True revival is a rebirth of piety and morality.

April 11   "The Revival of Religion Which We Need." At the Music Hall,
                Parker expressed his longing for a true revival of religion, a religion
                that is "the centermost of all delights." To know and follow "the
                Father and Mother of the world" is the greatest joy possible for
                human life. Most churches and ministers are guilty of promoting false
                religious revival, "belief in the theology of unreason, not a life of
                natural piety and morality." Parker referred to Emerson as the ideal
                promoter of true religion. "It is not doctrine he teaches . . . it is the
                inspiration of manliness that he imparts."

May 26   "The Relation of Slavery to a Republican Form of Government." In
                a speech delivered at the New England Anti-Slavery Convention in
                Boston, Parker declared slavery to be "inconsistent" with and "hostile"
                to a republican form of government. "It is clear what we ought to
                do," thundered Parker, the North must declare "slavery not to be
                tolerated in a republican form of government. No property in man.
                Immediate abolition. No slave state in the Union."

May 30–31   "The Biblical, the Ecclesiastical and the Philosophical Notion of God,
                and the Soul's Normal Delight in Him." Parker delivered four
                discourses on theology to the Yearly Meeting of Progressive Friends
                at Longwood, Pennsylvania: (1) "The Progressive Development of the
                Conception of God in the Books of the Bible;" (2) "The Ecclesiastical
                Conception of God, and Its Relation to the Scientific and Religious
                Wants of Man Now;" (3) "The Philosophical Idea of God and its
                Relation to the Scientific and Religious Wants of Mankind Now;" and
                (4) "The Soul's Normal Delight in the Infinite God."

Bibliography

WORKS BY THEODORE PARKER

An Address Delivered by the Rev. Theodore Parker, Before the New York City Anti-Slavery Society. New York: American Anti-Slavery Society, 1854.

An Anthology. Edited, with introduction and notes by Henry Steele Commager. Boston: Beacon Press, 1960.

The Biblical, the Ecclesiastical and the Philosophical Notion of God and the Soul's Normal Delight in Him. New York: John F. Trow, 1858.

The Boston Kidnapping: A Discourse to Commemorate the Rendition of Thomas Simms, Delivered on the First Anniversary Thereof, April 12, 1852. New York: Arno Press, 1969; repr. of 1852 ed.

Centenary Edition of the Works of Theodore Parker. 15 vols. Boston: American Unitarian Association, 1907–1910. Each volume bears a title of its own.

1. *A Discourse of Religion*
2. *Theism and Atheism*
3. *Sermons of Religion*
4. *Transient and Permanent*
5. *Matter and Man*
6. *Matter and Spirit*
7. *Historic Americans*
8. *The American Scholar*
9. *Sins and Safeguards*
10. *Social Classes in a Republic*
11. *The Slave Power*
12. *The Rights of Man*
13. *Autobiography, Poems and Prayers*
14. *Saint Bernard and Other Papers*
15. *Bibliography and Index*

The Collected Works of Theodore Parker. Frances P. Cobbe, ed. 14 vols. London: Trubner and Co., 1863. Each volume bears a title of its own.

1. *A Discourse of Matters Pertaining to Religion*
2. *Ten Sermons and Prayers*
3. *Discourses of Theology*
4. *Discourses of Politics*
5. *Discourses of Slavery*
6. *Discourses of Slavery*
7. *Discourses of Social Science*
8. *Miscellaneous Discourses*
9. *Critical and Miscellaneous*
10. *Critical and Miscellaneous*
11. *Theism, Atheism, and the Popular Theology*
12. *Miscellaneous*
13. *Historic Americans*
14. *Lessons From the World of Matter and the World of Men*

The Chief Sins of the People. Boston: Benjamin H. Greene, 1851. A sermon delivered at the Melodeon on Fast-Day, April 10, 1851.
The Critical and Miscellaneous Writings of Theodore Parker. Boston: J. Munroe and Co., 1843.
A Discourse Occasioned by the Death of Daniel Webster. Boston: B. B. Mussey and Co., 1853. Delivered at the Melodeon on October 31, 1852.
A Discourse of Matters Pertaining to Religion. Boston: Charles C. Little and James Brown, 1842.
The Effect of Slavery on the American People. Boston: W. L. Kent & Company, 1858. Sermon preached at the Music Hall, Sunday, July 4, 1858.
A False and True Revival of Religion. Boston: W. L. Kent & Company, 1858. Delivered at the Music Hall, April 4, 1858.
The Function and Place of Conscience in Relation to the Laws of Man: A Sermon For the Times. Boston: Crosby & Nichols, 1850. Delivered at the Melodeon, Sunday, September 22, 1850.
The Great Battle Between Slavery and Freedom. Boston: Benjamin H. Greene, 1856. From two speeches before the American Anti-Slavery Society.
John Brown's Expedition Reviewed in a Letter . . . to Francis Jackson. Boston: The Fraternity, 1860.
The Law of God and the Statutes of Men. Boston: Benjamin B. Mussey, 1854. Delivered at the Music Hall on Sunday, June 18, 1854.
A Letter to the People of the United States Touching the Matter of Slavery. Boston: James Munroe and Company, 1848.
Moral Dangers Incident to Prosperity. Boston: Benjamin H. Greene, 1855. Sermon delivered at the Music Hall on November 5, 1855.
The Nebraska Question. Some thoughts on the new assault upon freedom in America, and the general state of the country in relation thereunto, set forth in a discourse at the Music Hall. Boston: Benjamin B. Mussey & Co., 1854.
The New Crime Against Humanity. Boston: B. B. Mussey, 1854. A sermon on the fugitive slave, Anthony Burns, delivered at the Music Hall, Sunday, June 4, 1854.

A New Lesson For the Day. Boston: Benjamin H. Greene, 1856. Preached at the Music Hall, Sunday, May 25, 1856.

Prayers by Theodore Parker. A new edition with a preface by Louisa M. Alcott, and a memoir by F. B. Sanborn. Boston: Roberts Brothers, 1882.

The Present Aspect of Slavery in America and the Immediate Duty of the North. Boston: B. Marsh, 1858. A speech delivered in the Hall of the State House before the Massachusetts Anti-Slavery Convention on January 29, 1858.

The Public Education of the People. Boston: Wm. Crosby and H. P. Nichols, 1850. An oration delivered at the Onondaga Teachers' Institute at Syracuse, New York on October 4, 1849.

The Relation of Slavery to a Republican Form of Government. Boston: William L. Kent & Company, 1858. A speech delivered before the New England Anti-Slavery Convention on May 26, 1858.

The Revival of Religion Which We Need. Boston: William L. Kent, 1858. Delivered at the Music Hall, Sunday, April 11, 1858.

A Sermon of Merchants. Boston: by request, 1847. Preached at the Melodeon, Sunday, November 22, 1846.

A Sermon of the Consequences of an Immoral Principle and False Idea of Life. Boston: Benjamin H. Greene, 1855.

A Sermon of the Dangerous Classes in Society. Boston: C. & J.A. Spear, 1847.

A Sermon of the Dangers Which Threaten the Rights of Man in America. Boston: Benjamin B. Mussey & Co., 1854. Delivered at the Music Hall, Sunday, July 2, 1854.

A Sermon of Slavery. Boston: Thurston and Torry, 1843. Delivered on January 21 and repeated on June 4, 1843.

A Sermon on the Moral Condition of Boston. Boston: Crosby and Nichols, 1849. Delivered at the Melodeon, Sunday, February 11, 1849.

A Sermon on the Perishing Classes of Boston. Boston: I. R. Butts, 1846. Delivered at the Melodeon, August 30, 1846.

A Sermon on the Public Function of Women. Rochester: Curtis, Butts & Company, 1853. Delivered at the Music Hall, March 27, 1853.

A Sermon on the Spiritual Condition of Boston. Boston: Crosby and Nichols, 1849. A sermon delivered at the Melodeon on Sunday, February 18, 1849.

Speeches, Addresses, and Occasional Sermons. 3 vols. Boston: Horace B. Fuller, 1871.

The State of the Nation. Boston: Crosby and Nichols, 1851. A sermon for Thanksgiving Day, 1851.

Ten Sermons of Religion. Boston: Crosby, Nichols and Company, 1859.

Theism, Atheism, and the Popular Theology. London: John Chapman, 1853.

Theodore Parker's Experience As a Minister. Boston: Rufus Leighton, Jr., 1859.

Theodore Parker's Review of Webster. Boston: Redding and Company, 1850.

The Three Chief Safeguards of Society. Boston: Wm. Crosby and H. P. Nichols, 1851. Delivered at the Melodeon, Sunday, July 6, 1851.

The Trial of Theodore Parker for the "Misdemeanor" of a Speech in Faneuil Hall Against Kidnapping. Boston: Published for the author, 1855.

Views of Religion. Introduction by James Freeman Clarke. Boston: American Unitarian Association, 1885.

West Roxbury Sermons by Theodore Parker, 1837–1838. Samuel Barrows, ed. Boston: Roberts Brothers, 1892.

130   *Bibliography*

OTHER NINETEENTH-CENTURY SOURCES

Books

Broadus, John A. *On the Preparation and Delivery of Sermons*. New and revised edition by Jesse B. Weatherspoon. London: Hodder and Stoughton, 1949. Broadus first published this work in 1870.
Channing, W. E., ed. *Memoir of William Ellery Channing*. 3 vols. London: Routledge, 1850.
Dean, Peter. *The Life and Teachings of Theodore Parker*. London: Williams and Norgate, Ltd., 1877.
Frothingham, O. B. *Theodore Parker*. Boston: James R. Osgood and Co., 1874.
Lowell, James Russell. *A Fable For Critics, With Vignette Portraits of the Author De Quibus Fabula Narrator*. Freeport, NY: Books for Libraries Press, 1972; repr. of 1890 ed.
Reville, Albert. *The Life and Writings of Theodore Parker*. London: Simpkin, Marshall, and Co., 1865.
Ware, Henry Jr. *Hints on Extemporaneous Speaking*. Boston: Cummings, Hilliard and Co., 1824.
Weiss, John. *Life and Correspondence of Theodore Parker*. 2 vols. New York: D. Appleton and Company, 1864.

Newspapers

Richmond Examiner, November 6, 1842.
Streeter's Weekly Boston Star, April 11, 1846

TWENTIETH-CENTURY SOURCES

Books

Addison, Daniel Dulany. *The Clergy in American Life and Letters*. New York: The Macmillan Company, 1900.
Ahlstrom, Sydney E. *A Religious History of the American People*. New Haven: Yale University Press, 1972.
———, ed. *Theology in America: The Major Protestant Voices From Puritanism to Neo-Orthodoxy*. Indianapolis: Bobbs-Merrill Co., 1967.
Albrecht, Robert C. *Theodore Parker*. New York: Twayne Publishers, 1971.
Albright, Raymond W. *Focus on Infinity*. New York: The Macmillan Company, 1961.
Atkins, Gaius Glen, ed. *Master Sermons of the Nineteenth Century*. New York: Harper & Brothers, 1940.
Basler, Roy P., ed. *The Collected Works of Abraham Lincoln*. 9 vols. New Brunswick, NJ: Rutgers University Press, 1953.
Branch, Taylor. *Parting the Waters. America in the King Years, 1954–1963*. New York: Simon and Schuster, 1988.
Bratton, Fred Gladstone. *The Legacy of the Liberal Spirit*. New York: Charles Scribner's Sons, 1943.
Brigance, William Norwood, ed. *A History and Criticism of American Public Address*. 2 vols. New York: Russell & Russell, 1960.

Chadwick, John White. *Theodore Parker: Preacher and Reformer.* Boston: Houghton Mifflin Company, 1900.

———. *William Ellery Channing.* Boston: Houghton Mifflin Company, 1903.

Chandler, Daniel Ross. *The Rhetorical Tradition: Principles and Practice.* Boston: Kendall/Hunt Publishing Company, 1978.

Chesebrough, David B. *"God Ordained This War:" Sermons on the Sectional Crisis, 1830–1865.* Columbia, SC: University of South Carolina Press, 1991.

Clark, James Freeman. *A Look at the Life of Theodore Parker.* Boston: George H. Ellis Co., 1910.

Collins, Robert E., ed. *Theodore Parker: American Transcendentalist; A Critical Essay and a Collection of Writings.* Metuchen, NJ: Scarecrow Press, 1973.

Commager, Henry Steele. *Theodore Parker: An Anthology.* Boston: Beacon Press, 1960.

Commager, Henry Steele. *Theodore Parker: Yankee Crusader.* Boston: Little, Brown and Company, 1936.

Cooper, Lane. *The Rhetoric of Aristotle: An Expanded Translation With Supplementary Examples for Students of Composition and Public Speaking.* New York: Appleton-Century-Crofts, Inc., 1932.

Craven, Avery O. *Civil War in the Making, 1815–1860.* Baton Rouge: Louisiana State University Press, 1959.

Dirks, John Edward. *The Critical Theology of Theodore Parker.* New York: Columbia University Press, 1948.

Duffy, Bernard K. and Halford R. Ryan, eds. *American Orators Before 1900: Critical Studies and Sources.* Westport, CT: Greenwood Press, 1987.

Dunham, Chester Forrester. *The Attitude of the Northern Clergy Toward the South, 1860–1865.* Philadelphia: Porcupine Press, 1974.

Foner, Philip S., ed. *The Life and Writings of Frederick Douglass.* 5 vols. New York: International Publishers, 1950.

Frederickson, George M. *The Inner Civil War: Northern Intellectuals and the Crisis of the Union.* New York: Harper & Row, 1965.

Herndon, William J. and Jessie William Weik. *Herndon's Lincoln.* Springfield, IL: W. H. Herndon Publishing Company, 1921.

Hibben, Paxton. *Henry Ward Beecher: An American Portrait.* New York: Beekman Publishers, Inc., 1974; repr. of 1942 ed.

Holland, Dewitte, ed. *Preaching in American History.* Nashville: Abingdon Press, 1969.

———, ed. *Sermons in American History.* Nashville: Abingdon Press, 1971.

Howe, Daniel Parker. *The Unitarian Conscience: Harvard Moral Philosophy, 1805–1861.* Middleton, CT: Wesleyan University Press, 1988; repr. of 1970 ed. by Harvard University Press.

Hutchinson, William R. *The Transcendental Ministers: Church Reform in the New England Renaissance.* New Haven: Yale University Press, 1959.

King, Martin Luther Jr. *A Testament of Hope: The Essential Writings of Martin Luther King Jr.* James M. Washington, ed. San Francisco: Harper & Row, 1986.

McFeely, William S. *Frederick Douglass.* New York: W. W. Norton & Company, 1991.

McKivigan, John R. *The War Against Proslavery Religion: Abolitionism and the Northern Churches, 1830–1865.* Ithaca: Cornell University Press, 1984.

McLouglin, William G. *The Meaning of Henry Ward Beecher.* New York: Knopf, 1970.

McPherson, James M. *Abraham Lincoln and the Second American Revolution.* New York: Oxford University Press, 1991.

132   *Bibliography*

Miller, Perry. *The American Transcendentalists:* Garden City, NY: Anchor Books, 1957.
———, ed. *The Transcendentalists: An Anthology.* Cambridge: Harvard University Press, 1950.
Moorhead, James H. *American Apocalypse: Yankee Protestants and the Civil War.* New Haven: Yale University Press, 1978.
Oliver, Robert T. *History of Public Speaking in America.* Boston: Allyn and Bacon, Inc., 1965.
Reed, Thomas B. *Modern Eloquence.* 9 vols. Philadelphia: John D. Morris, 1900.
Richards, Laura E. and Maude Howe Elliot. *Julia Ward Howe, 1819–1910.* 2 vols. Boston: Houghton Mifflin Company, 1916.
Shaw, Warren C. *History of American Oratory.* Indianapolis: Bobbs-Merrill, 1928.
Sherwin, Oscar. *Prophet of Liberty: The Life and Times of Wendell Phillips.* New York: Bookman Associates, 1958.
Smith, J. W. and A. L. Jamison, eds. *The Shaping of American Religion.* Princeton: Princeton University Press, 1961.
Williams, George. *Rethinking the Unitarian Relationship With Protestantism.* Boston: Beacon Press, 1949.
Wills, Garry. *Lincoln at Gettysburg: The Words That Remade America.* New York: Simon & Schuster, 1992.
Wright, Conrad, ed. *Three Prophets of Religious Liberalism: Channing, Emerson, Parker.* Boston: Unitarian Universalist Association, 1986.

Articles

Ahlstrom, Sydney. "Theology in America: A Historical Survey." *The Shaping of American Religion.* J. W. Smith and A. L. Jamison, eds. Princeton: Princeton University Press, pp. 1:232–321.
Chandler, David Ross. "Octavius Brooks Frothingham: The Religion of Humanity." *Religious Humanism* 19 (1985), pp. 102–110, 154–65.
———. "Theodore Parker (1810–1860), Unitarian Clergyman." *American Orators Before 1900: Critical Studies and Sources.* Bernard K. Duffy and Halford R. Ryan, eds. Westport, CT: Greenwood Press, 1987. pp. 307–15.
Chesebrough, David B. "The Civil War and the Use of Sermons as Historical Documents." *Organization of American Historians Magazine of History.* 8 (Fall 1993): pp. 26–29.
Harrington, Donald S. "Theodore Parker, Crusader." *The Rhetorical Tradition: Principles and Practice.* Daniel Ross Chandler. Boston: Kendall/Hunt Publishing Company, 1978. pp. 158–67.
Hochmuth, Marie and Norman W. Mattis. "Phillips Brooks." *A History and Criticism of American Public Address.* 2 vols. William Norwood Brigance, ed. New York: Russell & Russell, 1960. pp. 1:294–328.
McCall, Roy C. "Theodore Parker." *A History and Criticism of American Public Address.* William Norwood Brigance, ed. New York: Russell & Russell, 1960. pp. 1:238–264.
Teed, Paul. "Racial Nationalism and Its Challengers: Theodore Parker, John Rock, and the Antislavery Movement." *Civil War History.* 41 (June 1995): 142–60.

Unpublished Dissertations

Chesebrough, David B. "The Call to Battle: The Stances of Parker, Finney, Beecher, and Brooks on the Great Issues Surrounding the Civil War and a Comparison of Those Stances With Other Clergy in the Nation." Doctoral dissertation, Illinois State University, 1988.

Lambertson, F. W. A. "A Survey and Analysis of American Homiletic Theory Prior to 1860." Doctoral dissertation, University of Iowa, 1930.

Index

ABOUT THE AUTHOR

DAVID B. CHESEBROUGH is a member of the graduate faculty in the department of history at Illinois State University. He has published *God Ordained this War* (1991), *No Sorrow Like Our Sorrow* (1994), *Clergy Dissent in the Old South* (1996), and most recently *Frederick Douglass: Oratory from Slavery* (Greenwood, 1998).

GREAT AMERICAN ORATORS

Mark Twain: Protagonist for the Popular Culture
Marlene Boyd Vallin

Delightful Conviction: Jonathan Edwards and the Rhetoric of Conversion
Stephen R. Yarbrough and John C. Adams

Harry S. Truman: Presidential Rhetoric
Halford R. Ryan

Dwight D. Eisenhower: Strategic Communicator
Martin J. Medhurst

Ralph Waldo Emerson: Preacher and Lecturer
Lloyd Rohler

"In a Perilous Hour": The Public Address of John F. Kennedy
Steven R. Goldzwig and George N. Dionisopoulos

Douglas MacArthur: Warrior as Wordsmith
Bernard K. Duffy and Ronald H. Carpenter

Sojourner Truth as Orator: Wit, Story, and Song
Suzanne Pullon Fitch and Roseann M. Mandziuk

Frederick Douglass: Oratory from Slavery
David B. Chesebrough

Father Charles E. Coughlin: Surrogate Spokesperson for the Disaffected
Ronald H. Carpenter

Margaret Chase Smith: Model Public Servant
Marlene Boyd Vallin

Helen Keller, Public Speaker: Sightless But Seen, Deaf But Heard
Lois J. Einhorn

www.ingramcontent.com/pod-product-compliance
Lightning Source LLC
Chambersburg PA
CBHW020400100426
42812CB00001B/130